MW00916589

THIS BOOK

BELONGS TO

WHAT SHOULD WE DRAW TODAY?

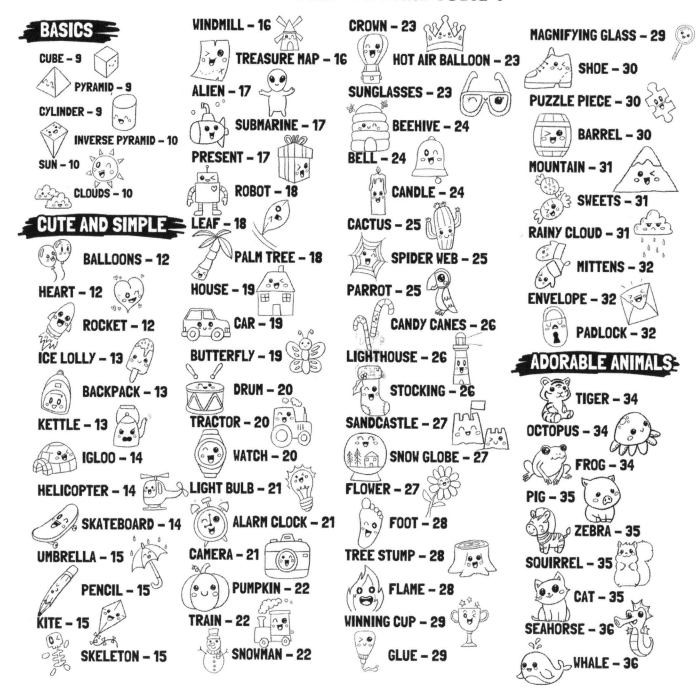

BASICS

- CUBE – 9
- PYRAMID – 9
- CYLINDER – 9
- INVERSE PYRAMID – 10
- SUN – 10
- CLOUDS – 10

CUTE AND SIMPLE

- BALLOONS – 12
- HEART – 12
- ROCKET – 12
- ICE LOLLY – 13
- BACKPACK – 13
- KETTLE – 13
- IGLOO – 14
- HELICOPTER – 14
- SKATEBOARD – 14
- UMBRELLA – 15
- PENCIL – 15
- KITE – 15
- SKELETON – 15

- WINDMILL – 16
- TREASURE MAP – 16
- ALIEN – 17
- SUBMARINE – 17
- PRESENT – 17
- ROBOT – 18
- LEAF – 18
- PALM TREE – 18
- HOUSE – 19
- CAR – 19
- BUTTERFLY – 19
- DRUM – 20
- TRACTOR – 20
- WATCH – 20
- LIGHT BULB – 21
- ALARM CLOCK – 21
- CAMERA – 21
- PUMPKIN – 22
- TRAIN – 22
- SNOWMAN – 22

- CROWN – 23
- HOT AIR BALLOON – 23
- SUNGLASSES – 23
- BEEHIVE – 24
- BELL – 24
- CANDLE – 24
- CACTUS – 25
- SPIDER WEB – 25
- PARROT – 25
- CANDY CANES – 26
- LIGHTHOUSE – 26
- STOCKING – 26
- SANDCASTLE – 27
- SNOW GLOBE – 27
- FLOWER – 27
- FOOT – 28
- TREE STUMP – 28
- FLAME – 28
- WINNING CUP – 29
- GLUE – 29

- MAGNIFYING GLASS – 29
- SHOE – 30
- PUZZLE PIECE – 30
- BARREL – 30
- MOUNTAIN – 31
- SWEETS – 31
- RAINY CLOUD – 31
- MITTENS – 32
- ENVELOPE – 32
- PADLOCK – 32

ADORABLE ANIMALS

- TIGER – 34
- OCTOPUS – 34
- FROG – 34
- PIG – 35
- ZEBRA – 35
- SQUIRREL – 35
- CAT – 35
- SEAHORSE – 36
- WHALE – 36

WHAT SHOULD WE DRAW TODAY?

DUCK – 37
PANDA – 37
STARFISH – 37
FISH – 38
EAGLE – 38
LADYBUG – 38
NARWHAL – 39
CATERPILLAR – 39
ANTELOPE – 39
CHICKEN – 40
HIPPO – 40
KOALA – 40
PENGUIN – 41
MONKEY – 41
COW – 41
SHEEP – 42
FOX – 42
TURTLE – 42
DOG – 43
BEE – 43

RABBIT – 43
FLAMINGO – 44
RHINO – 44
GOAT – 44
SPIDER – 45
DEER – 45
HAMSTER – 45
OWL – 46
WOLF – 46
CAMEL – 46
SNAIL – 47
POLAR BEAR – 47
SWAN – 47
ELEPHANT – 48
RACCOON – 48
DOE – 48
GOOSE – 49
LLAMA – 49
MOSQUITO – 49
CROCODILE – 50

STORK – 50
DOLPHIN – 50
SHARK – 51
KANGAROO – 51
PUPPY – 51
LION – 52
MOOSE – 52
ANT – 52
BAT – 53
LOBSTER – 53
PEACOCK – 53
BUFFALO – 54
SEAL – 54
GORILLA – 54
TURKEY – 55
DANCING DUCK – 55
GUINEA PIG – 55
OTTER – 56
SNAKE – 56
MOUSE – 56

SLOTH – 57
AARDVARK – 57
OSTRICH – 57
VULTURE – 58
WARTHOG – 58
ANTEATER – 58

LOVEABLE FOOD

TACO – 60
CROISSANT – 60
STRAWBERRY – 60
PIZZA – 61
APPLE – 61
CHEESE – 61
BURGER – 62
HOT DOG – 62
ICE CREAM – 62
PANCAKE – 63
DONUT – 63
WATERMELON – 63
FRIED EGG – 64

WHAT SHOULD WE DRAW TODAY?

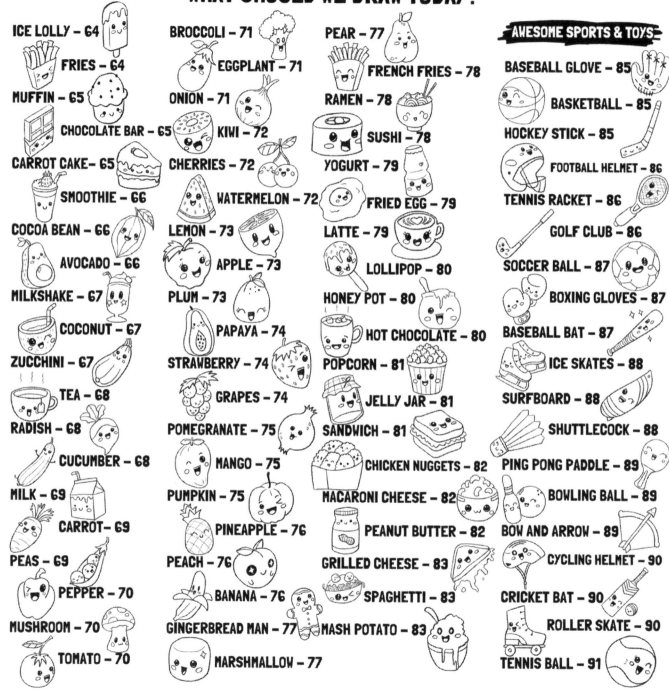

ICE LOLLY – 64
FRIES – 64
MUFFIN – 65
CHOCOLATE BAR – 65
CARROT CAKE– 65
SMOOTHIE – 66
COCOA BEAN – 66
AVOCADO – 66
MILKSHAKE – 67
COCONUT – 67
ZUCCHINI – 67
TEA – 68
RADISH – 68
CUCUMBER – 68
MILK – 69
CARROT– 69
PEAS – 69
PEPPER – 70
MUSHROOM – 70
TOMATO – 70

BROCCOLI – 71
EGGPLANT – 71
ONION – 71
KIWI – 72
CHERRIES – 72
WATERMELON – 72
LEMON – 73
APPLE – 73
PLUM – 73
PAPAYA – 74
STRAWBERRY – 74
GRAPES – 74
POMEGRANATE – 75
MANGO – 75
PUMPKIN – 75
PINEAPPLE – 76
PEACH – 76
BANANA – 76
GINGERBREAD MAN – 77
MARSHMALLOW – 77

PEAR – 77
FRENCH FRIES – 78
RAMEN – 78
SUSHI – 78
YOGURT – 79
FRIED EGG – 79
LATTE – 79
LOLLIPOP – 80
HONEY POT – 80
HOT CHOCOLATE – 80
POPCORN – 81
JELLY JAR – 81
SANDWICH – 81
CHICKEN NUGGETS – 82
MACARONI CHEESE – 82
PEANUT BUTTER – 82
GRILLED CHEESE – 83
SPAGHETTI – 83
MASH POTATO – 83

AWESOME SPORTS & TOYS

BASEBALL GLOVE – 85
BASKETBALL – 85
HOCKEY STICK – 85
FOOTBALL HELMET – 86
TENNIS RACKET – 86
GOLF CLUB – 86
SOCCER BALL – 87
BOXING GLOVES – 87
BASEBALL BAT – 87
ICE SKATES – 88
SURFBOARD – 88
SHUTTLECOCK – 88
PING PONG PADDLE – 89
BOWLING BALL – 89
BOW AND ARROW – 89
CYCLING HELMET – 90
CRICKET BAT – 90
ROLLER SKATE – 90
TENNIS BALL – 91

WHAT SHOULD WE DRAW TODAY?

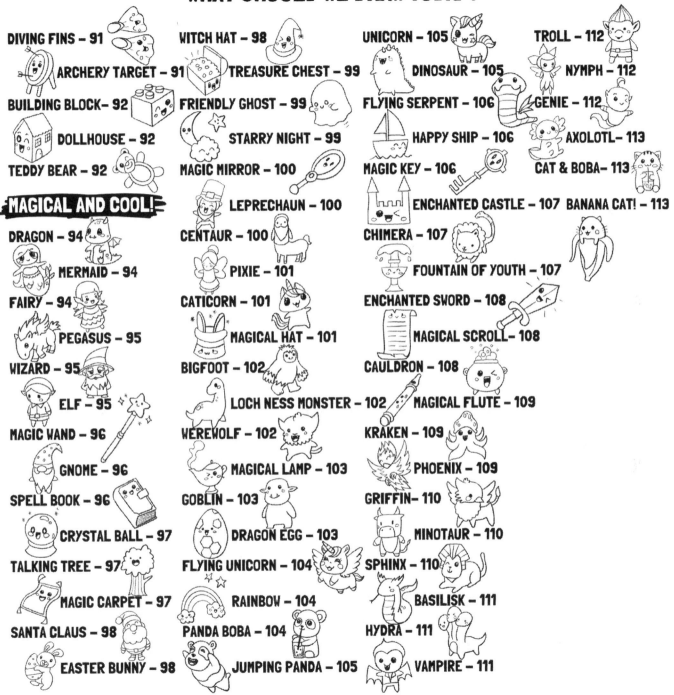

DIVING FINS – 91

ARCHERY TARGET – 91

BUILDING BLOCK– 92

DOLLHOUSE – 92

TEDDY BEAR – 92

MAGICAL AND COOL!

DRAGON – 94

MERMAID – 94

FAIRY – 94

PEGASUS – 95

WIZARD – 95

ELF – 95

MAGIC WAND – 96

GNOME – 96

SPELL BOOK – 96

CRYSTAL BALL – 97

TALKING TREE – 97

MAGIC CARPET – 97

SANTA CLAUS – 98

EASTER BUNNY – 98

WITCH HAT – 98

TREASURE CHEST – 99

FRIENDLY GHOST – 99

STARRY NIGHT – 99

MAGIC MIRROR – 100

LEPRECHAUN – 100

CENTAUR – 100

PIXIE – 101

CATICORN – 101

MAGICAL HAT – 101

BIGFOOT – 102

LOCH NESS MONSTER – 102

WEREWOLF – 102

MAGICAL LAMP – 103

GOBLIN – 103

DRAGON EGG – 103

FLYING UNICORN – 104

RAINBOW – 104

PANDA BOBA – 104

JUMPING PANDA – 105

UNICORN – 105

DINOSAUR – 105

FLYING SERPENT – 106

HAPPY SHIP – 106

MAGIC KEY – 106

ENCHANTED CASTLE – 107

CHIMERA – 107

FOUNTAIN OF YOUTH – 107

ENCHANTED SWORD – 108

MAGICAL SCROLL– 108

CAULDRON – 108

MAGICAL FLUTE – 109

KRAKEN – 109

PHOENIX – 109

GRIFFIN– 110

MINOTAUR – 110

SPHINX – 110

BASILISK – 111

HYDRA – 111

VAMPIRE – 111

TROLL – 112

NYMPH – 112

GENIE – 112

AXOLOTL– 113

CAT & BOBA– 113

BANANA CAT! – 113

WELCOME TO YOUR NEW DRAWING BOOK!

INSIDE, YOU'LL FIND 300 SUPER CUTE THINGS TO DRAW. FOLLOW THE EASY 6-STEP GUIDES TO CREATE EACH PICTURE. WE'LL BEGIN WITH SIMPLE SHAPES AND CONTINUE TO ALL SORTS OF FUN THINGS LIKE ANIMALS, FOOD, AND MAGICAL CREATURES! LET'S GET STARTED!

WHAT YOU NEED TO GET STARTED:

JUST A PENCIL!

AND THESE ARE OPTIONAL:

PAPER

COLOR PENCILS

ERASER

HOW TO USE THIS BOOK

EVERY PAGE HAS THREE AMAZING THINGS TO DRAW!

THERE'S ROOM FOR YOU TO PRACTICE!

EACH WITH SIX EASY STEPS TO FOLLOW.

DUCK — PRACTICE

PANDA — PRACTICE

STARFISH — PRACTICE

TAKE AS MUCH TIME AS YOU NEED, AND ABOVE ALL, ENJOY YOURSELF!

LET'S DRAW!

LET'S KICK THINGS OFF WITH SOMETHING SIMPLE. A CUBE!

GIVE IT A GO HERE

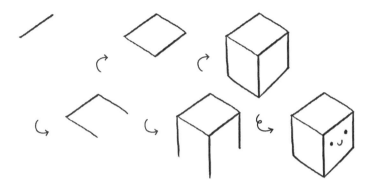

HOW ABOUT WE GIVE A PYRAMID A WHIRL?

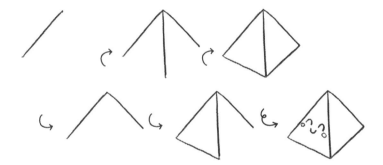

GOOD JOB! LET'S TRY SOMETHING A BIT MORE CHALLENGING: A CYLINDER.

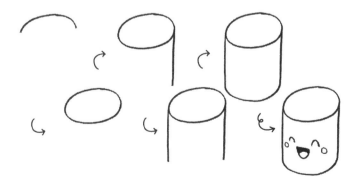

FEELING AWESOME?! HOW ABOUT TRYING YOUR HAND AT AN INVERSE PYRAMID?

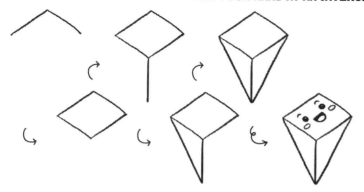

DOING GREAT! LET'S MAKE THINGS MORE INTERESTING.

NOW TRY SOME CLOUDS!

WOW! YOU SMASHED IT! IT'S TIME TO DRAW, GOOD LUCK AND REMEMBER TO HAVE FUN!

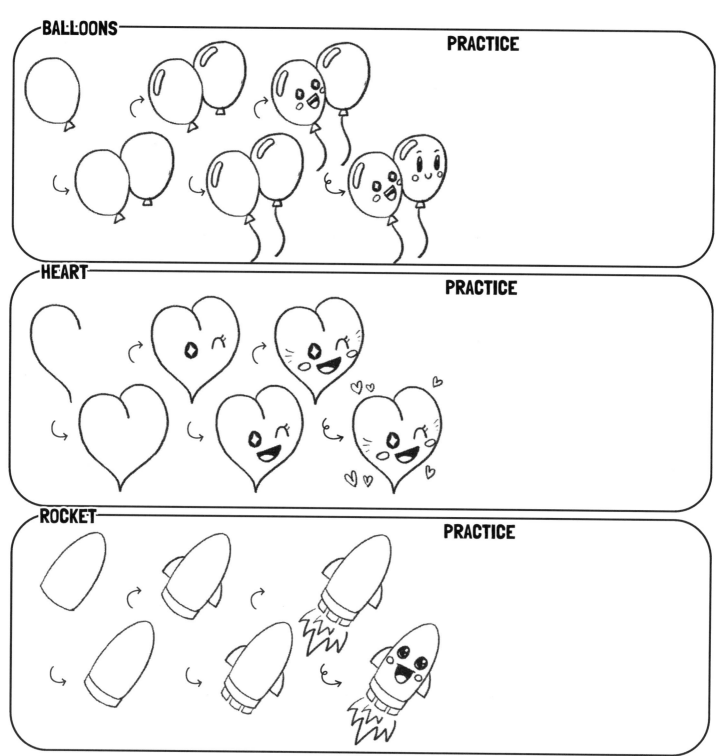

BALLOONS

PRACTICE

HEART

PRACTICE

ROCKET

PRACTICE

ICE-LOLLY

BACKPACK

KETTLE

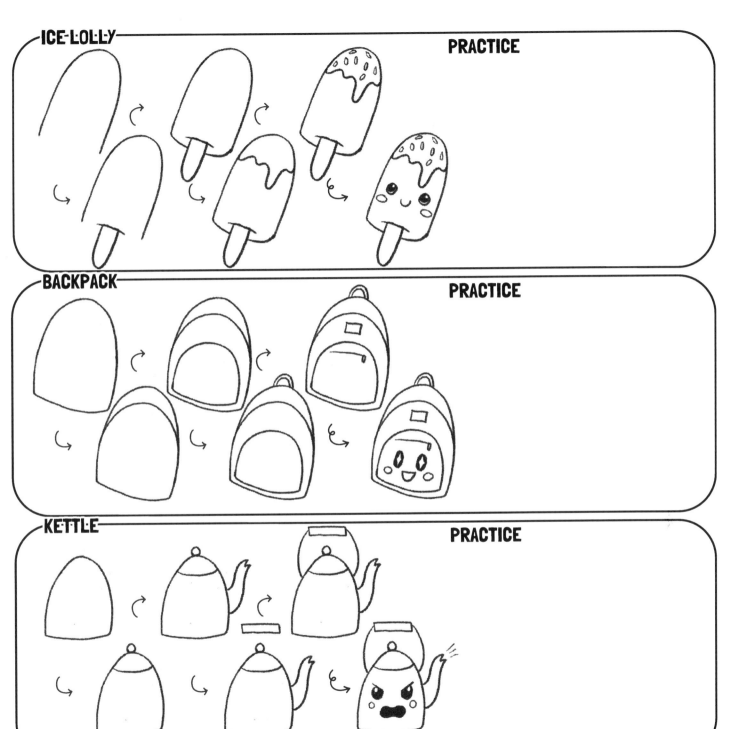

IGLOO

HELICOPTER

SKATEBOARD

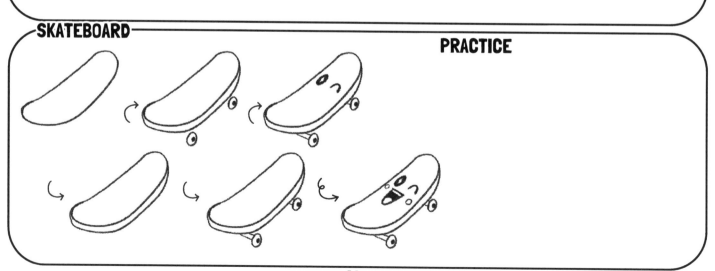

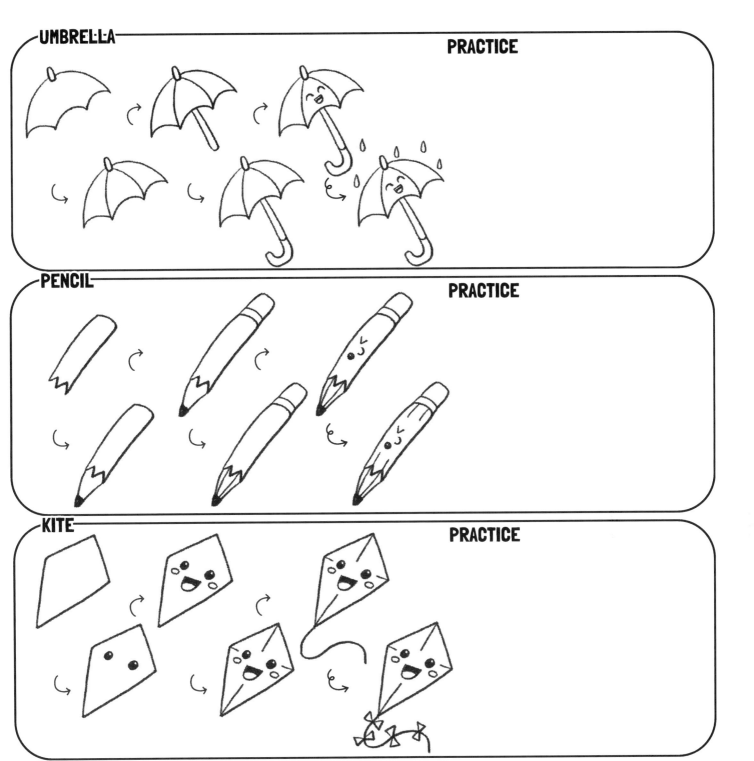

UMBRELLA   PRACTICE

PENCIL   PRACTICE

KITE   PRACTICE

15

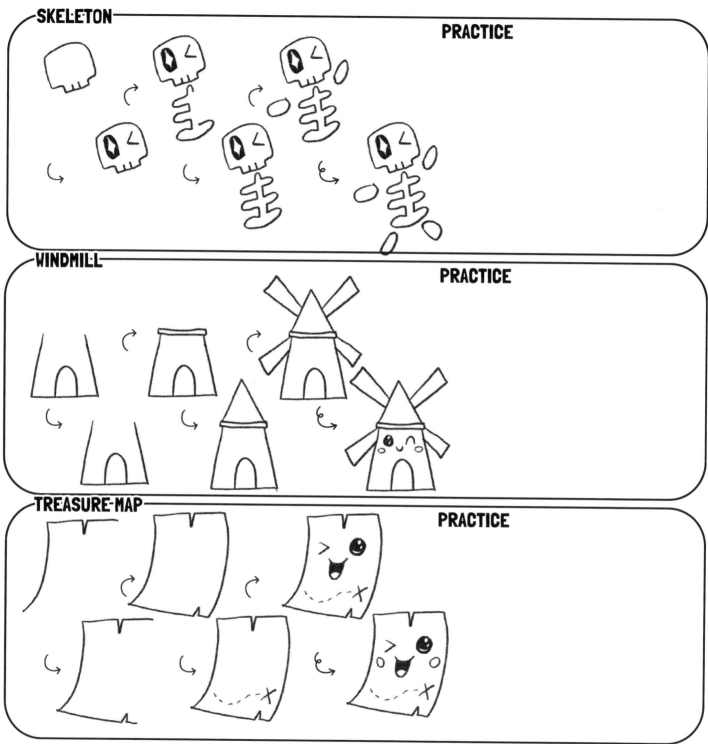

SKELETON
PRACTICE

WINDMILL
PRACTICE

TREASURE-MAP
PRACTICE

ALIEN

SUBMARINE

PRESENT

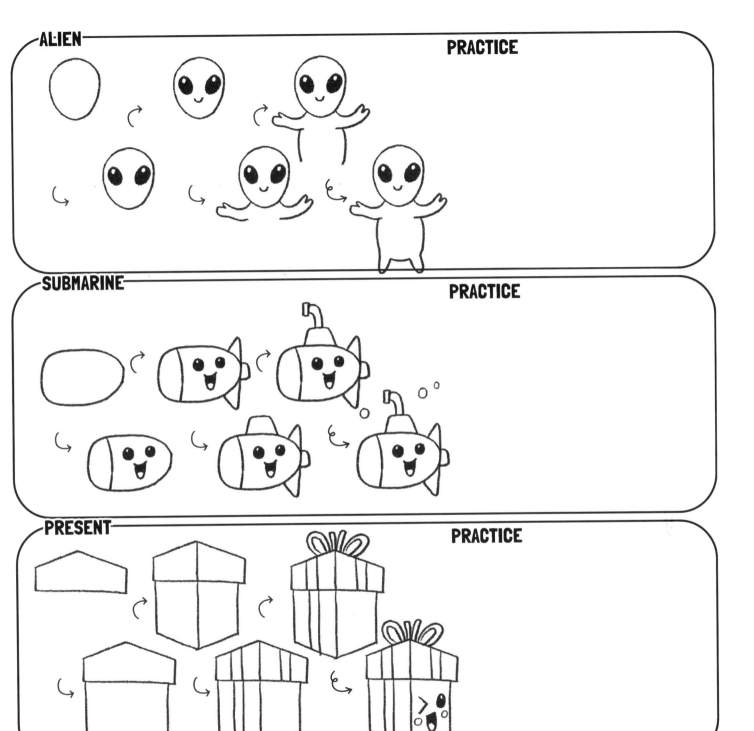

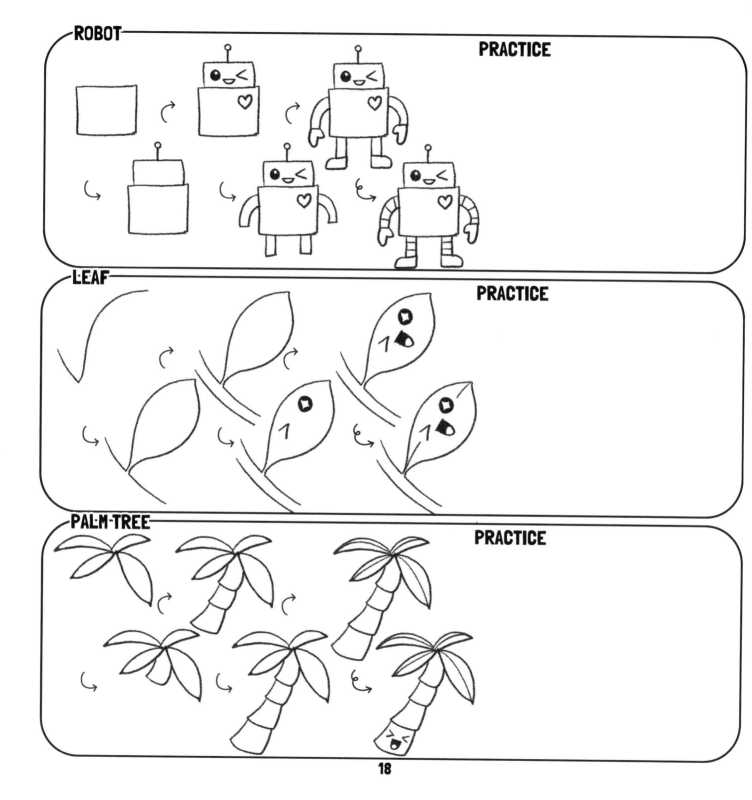

ROBOT PRACTICE

LEAF PRACTICE

PALM-TREE PRACTICE

18

HOUSE

CAR

BUTTERFLY

LIGHT BULB

ALARM CLOCK

CAMERA

PUMPKIN

TRAIN

SNOWMAN

CROWN

HOT-AIR BALLOON

SUNGLASSES

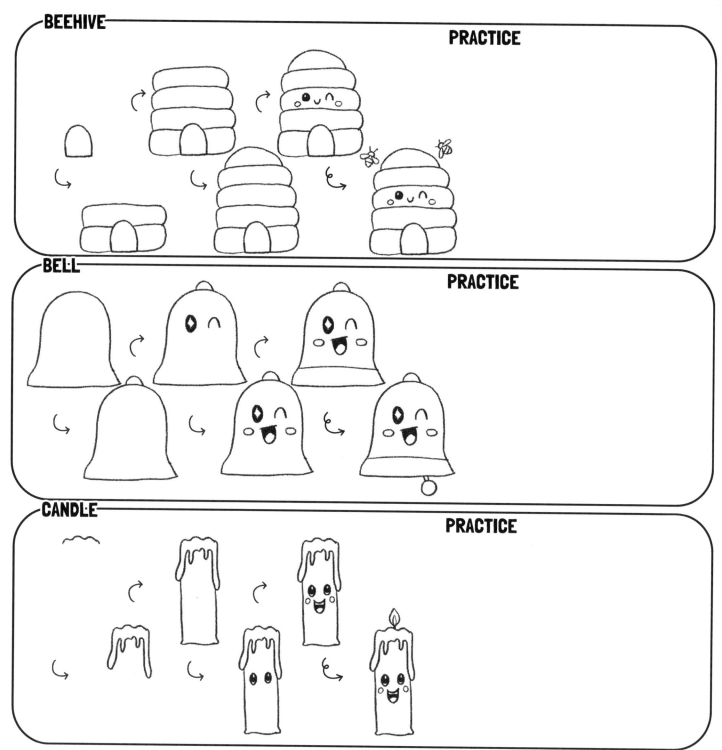

BEEHIVE

PRACTICE

BELL

PRACTICE

CANDLE

PRACTICE

24

CACTUS

SPIDER WEB

PARROT

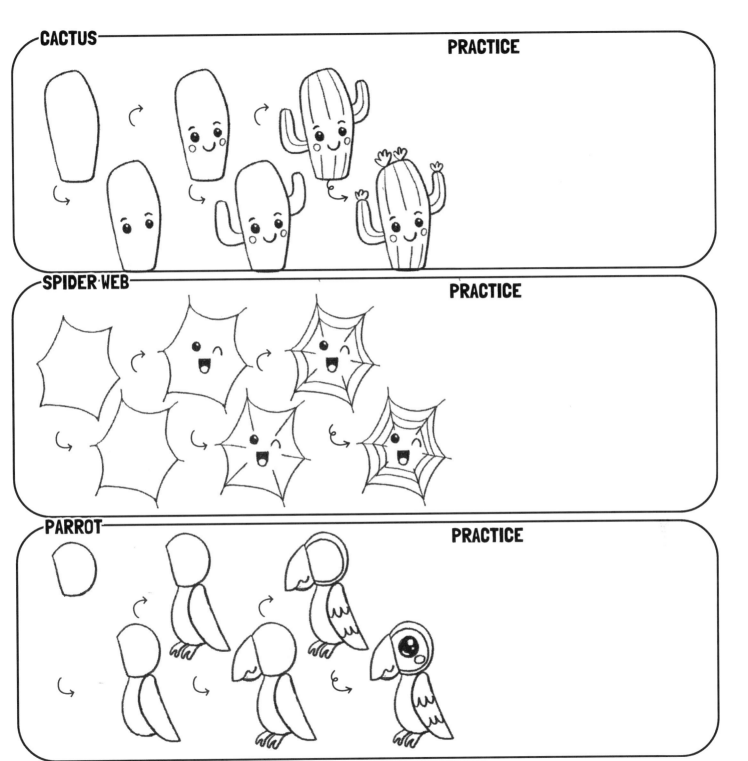

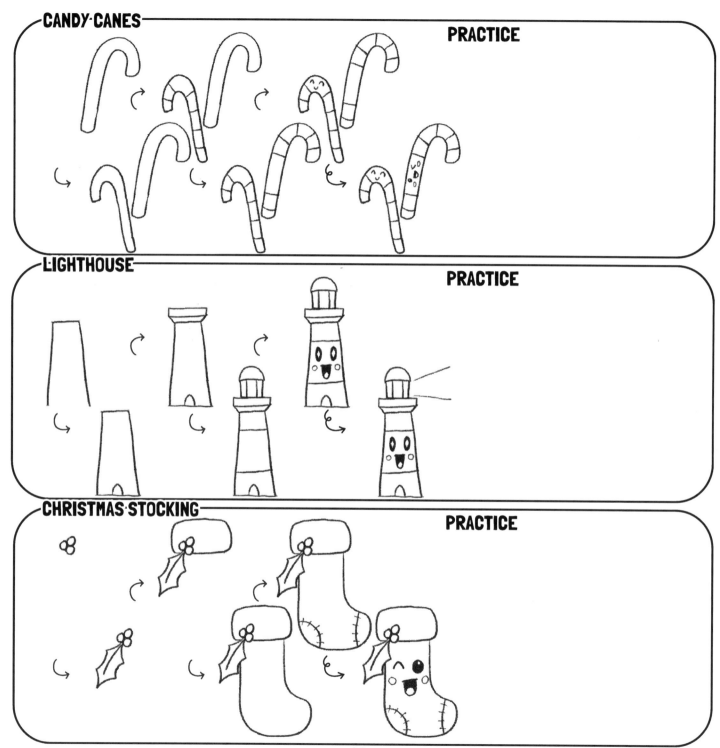

SANDCASTLE

SNOW GLOBE

FLOWER

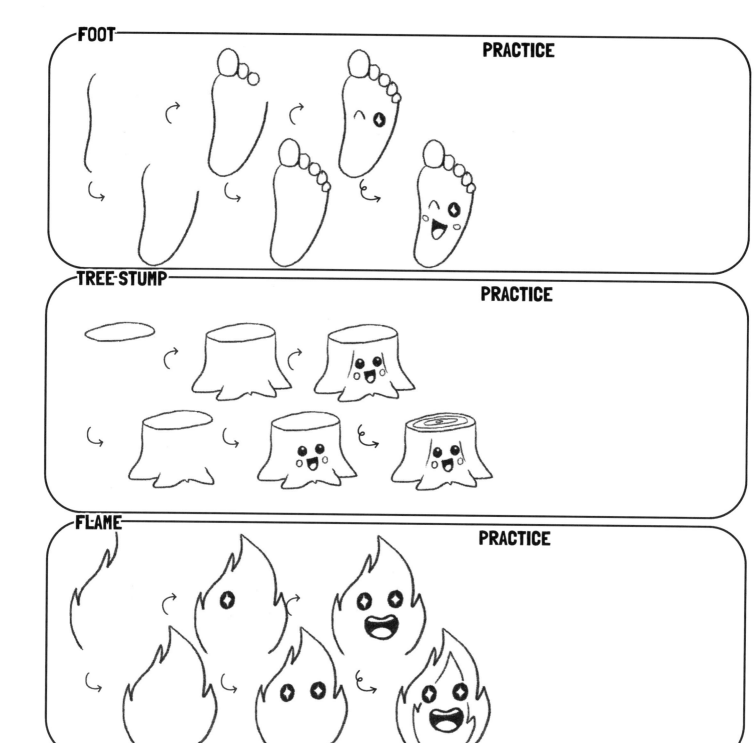

FOOT

PRACTICE

TREE-STUMP

PRACTICE

FLAME

PRACTICE

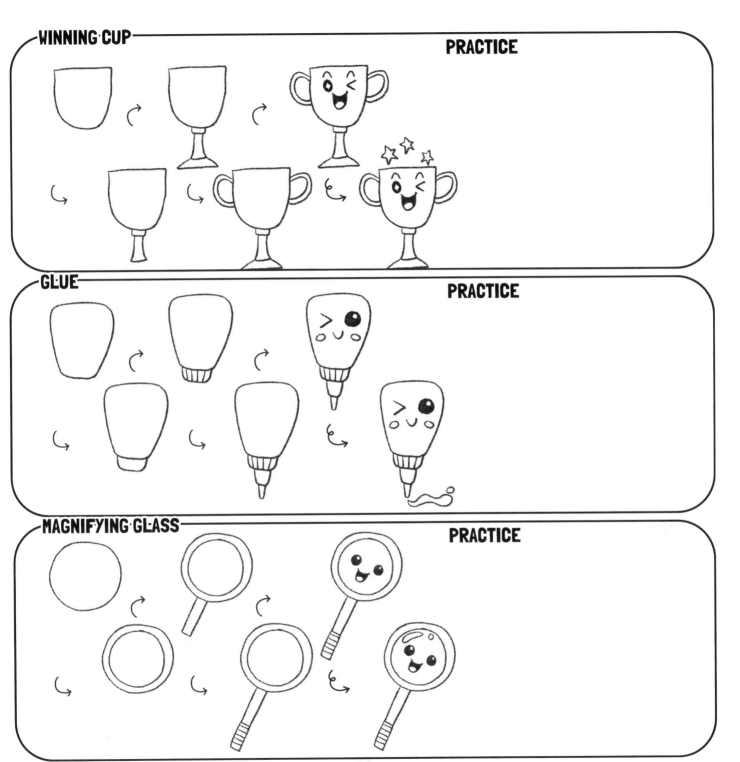

WINNING·CUP

PRACTICE

GLUE

PRACTICE

MAGNIFYING·GLASS

PRACTICE

SHOE

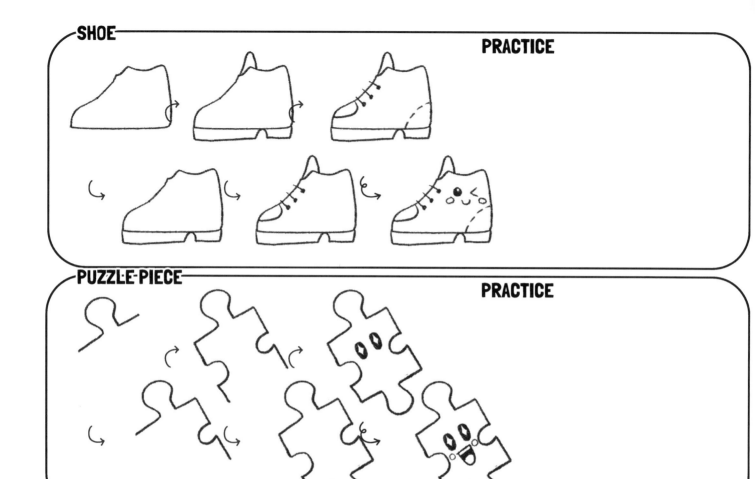

PUZZLE PIECE

PRACTICE

BARREL

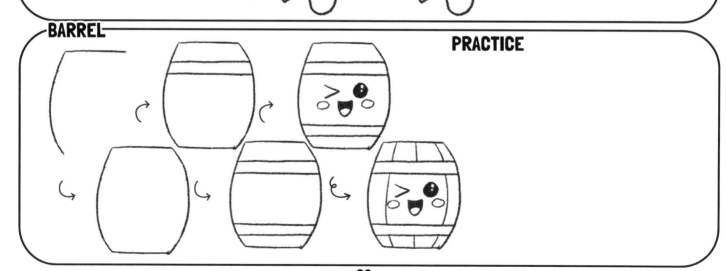

PRACTICE

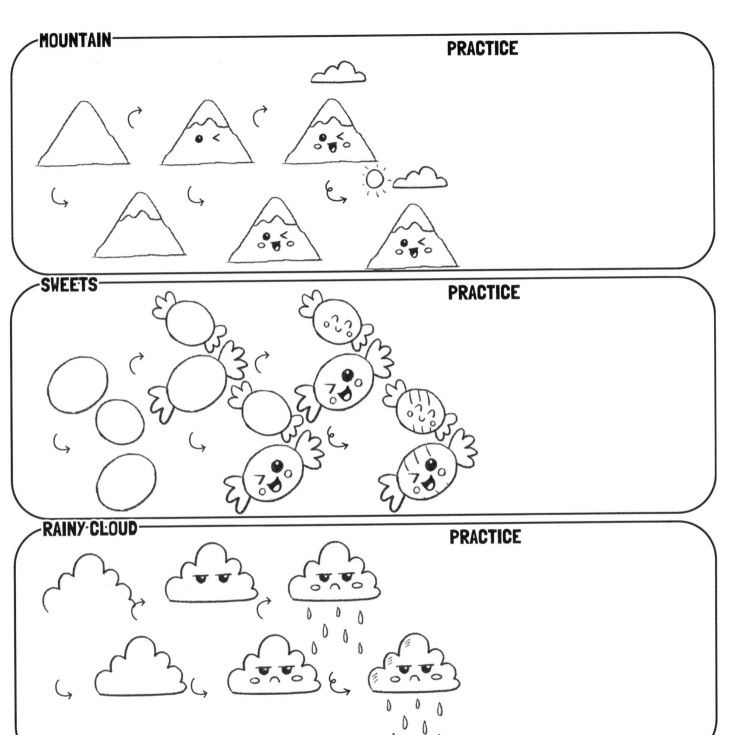

MOUNTAIN

SWEETS

RAINY·CLOUD

ADORABLE ANIMALS

TIGER

OCTOPUS

FROG

PIG

ZEBRA

SQUIRREL

CAT

PRACTICE

SEAHORSE

PRACTICE

WHALE

PRACTICE

DUCK

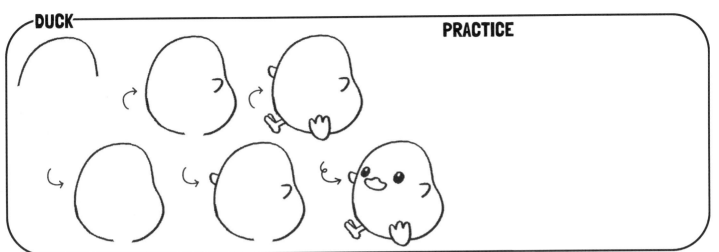

PANDA

STARFISH

FISH

EAGLE

LADYBUG

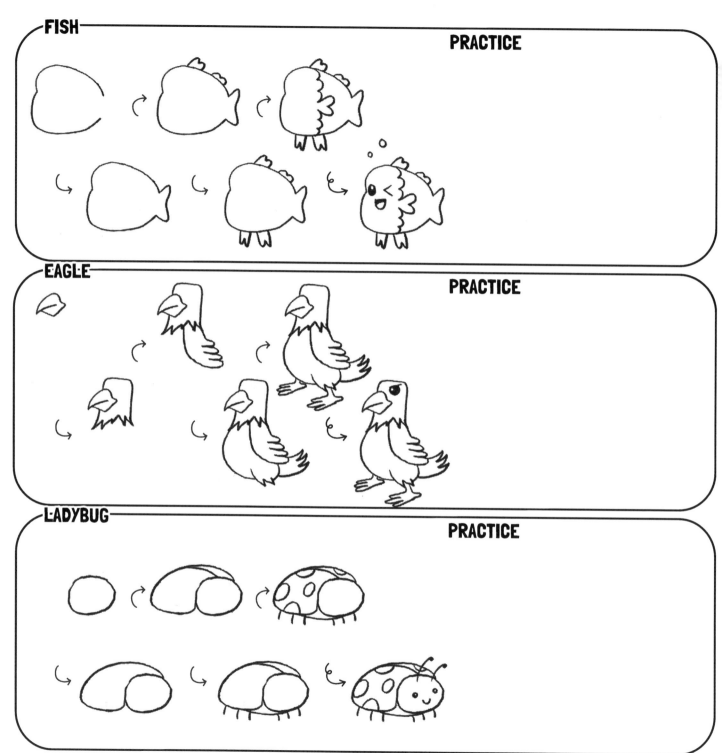

NARWHAL

CATERPILLAR

ANTELOPE

CHICKEN

HIPPO

KOALA

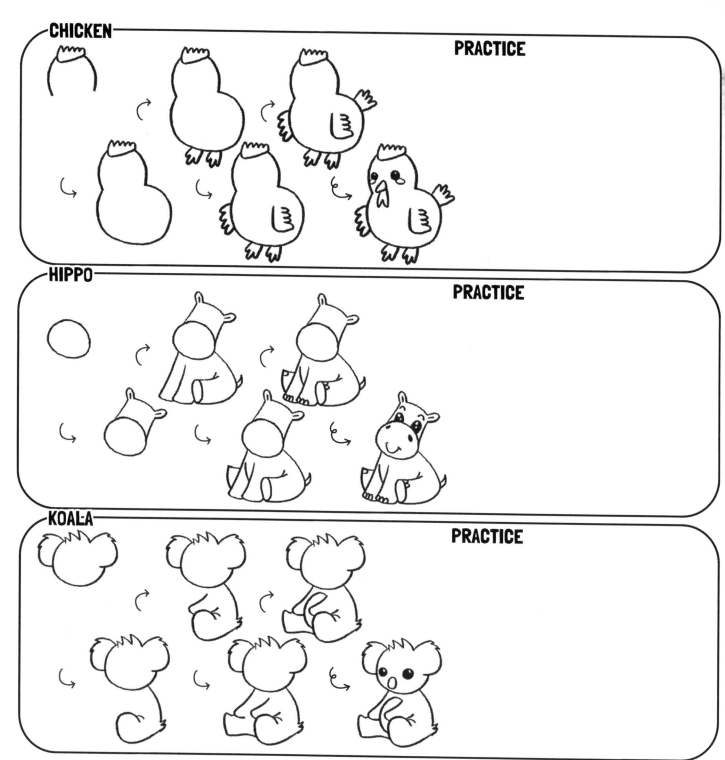

PENGUIN

PRACTICE

MONKEY

PRACTICE

COW

PRACTICE

41

SHEEP

FOX

TURTLE

DOG

BEE

RABBIT

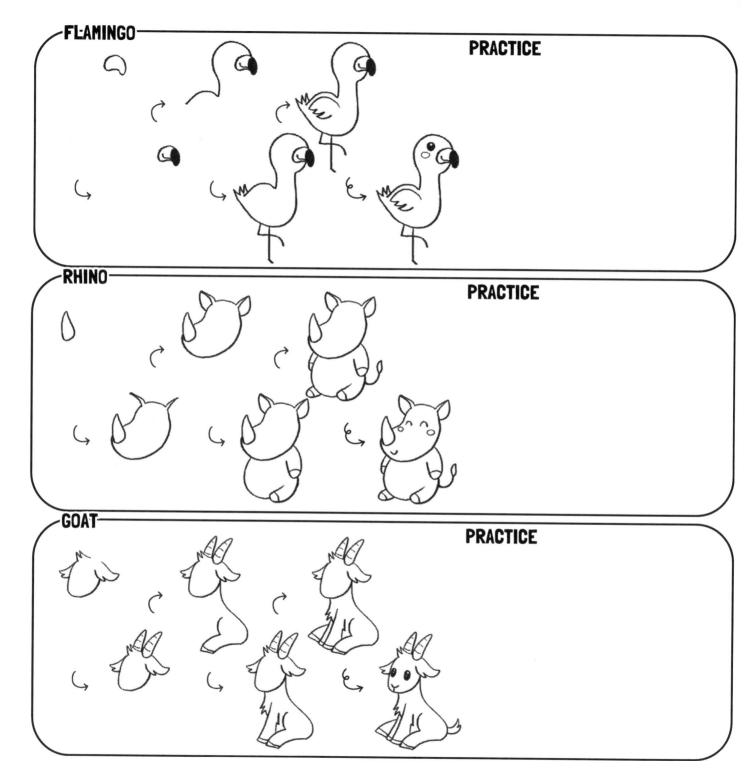

FLAMINGO PRACTICE

RHINO PRACTICE

GOAT PRACTICE

44

SPIDER

DEER

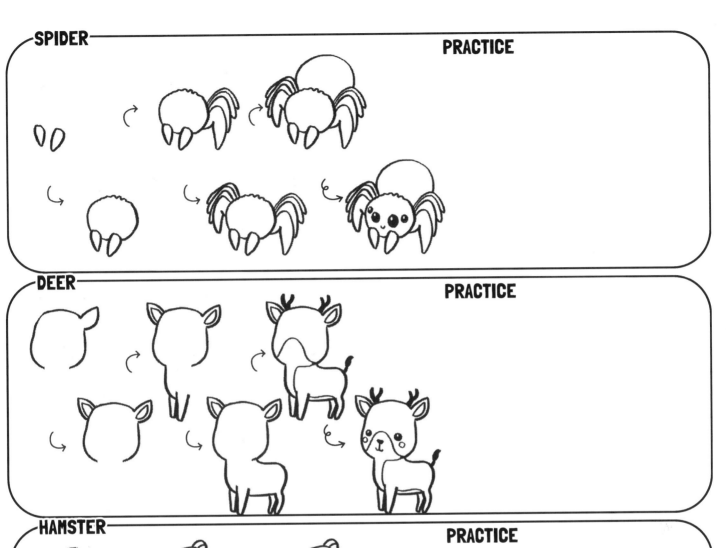

HAMSTER

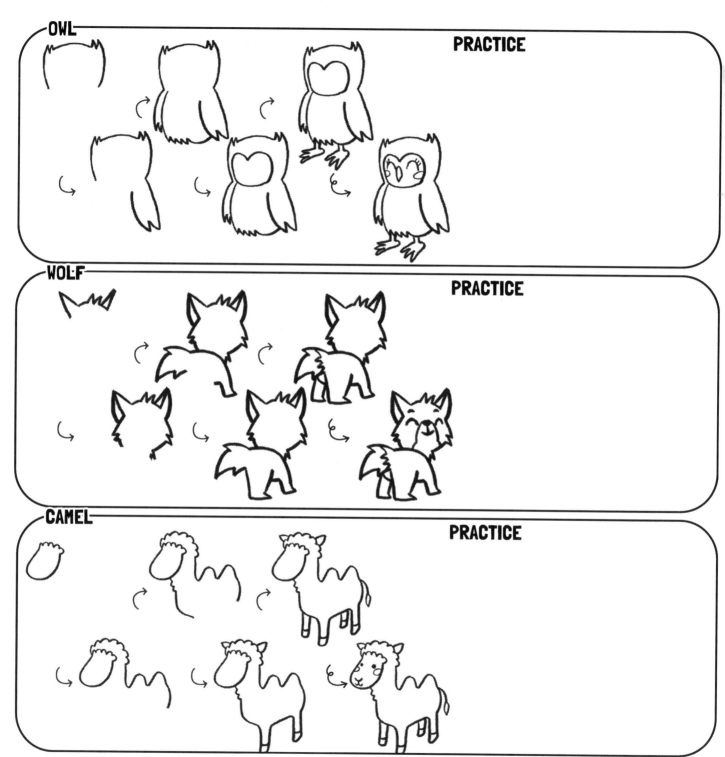

SNAIL

POLAR BEAR

SWAN

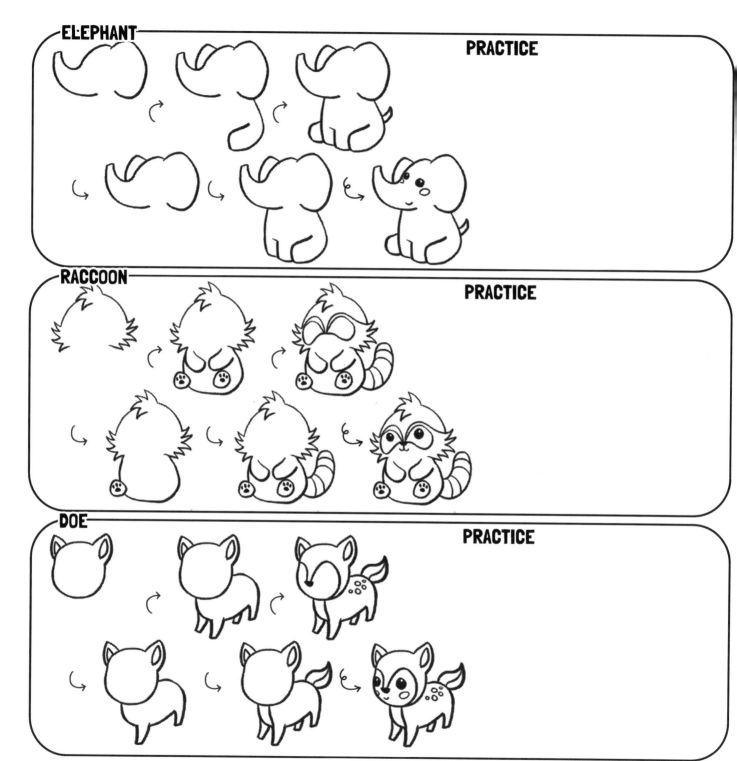

ELEPHANT PRACTICE

RACCOON PRACTICE

DOE PRACTICE

48

GOOSE

LLAMA

MOSQUITO

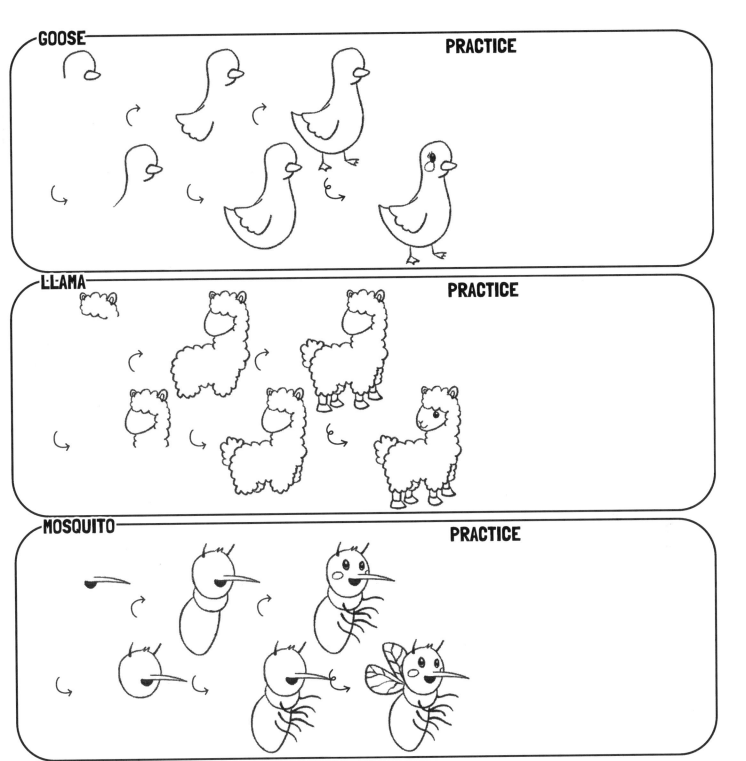

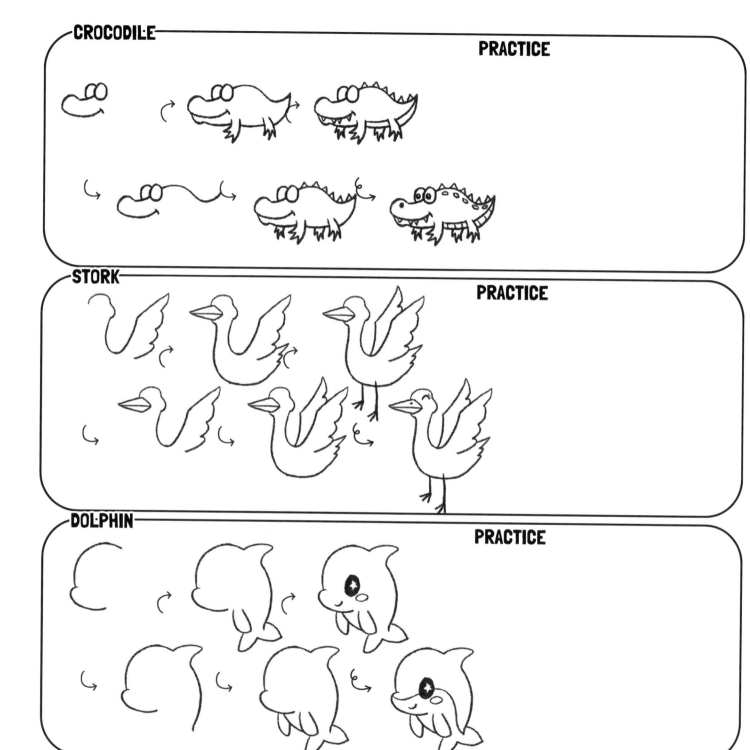

CROCODILE

PRACTICE

STORK

PRACTICE

DOLPHIN

PRACTICE

SHARK — PRACTICE

KANGAROO — PRACTICE

PUPPY — PRACTICE

LION

MOOSE

ANT

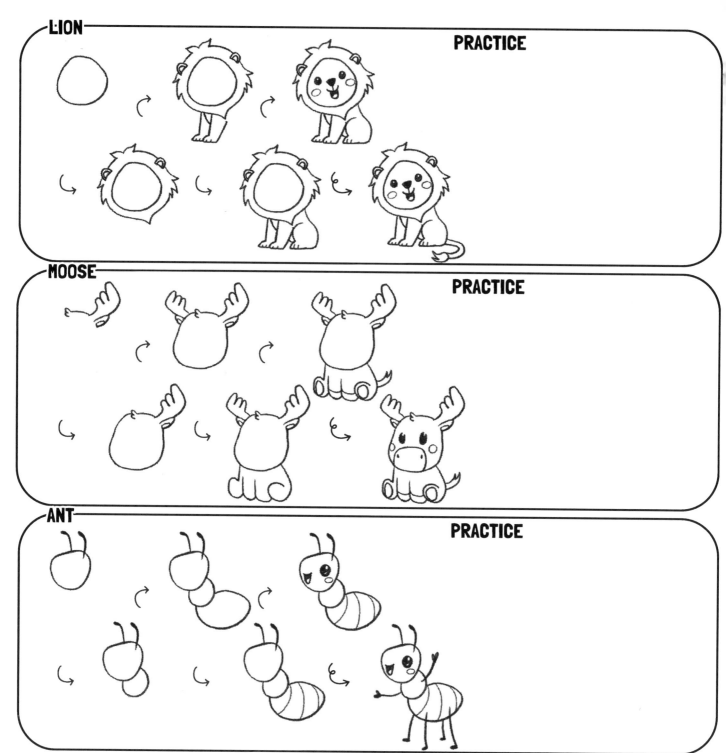

BAT

LOBSTER

PEACOCK

BUFFALO

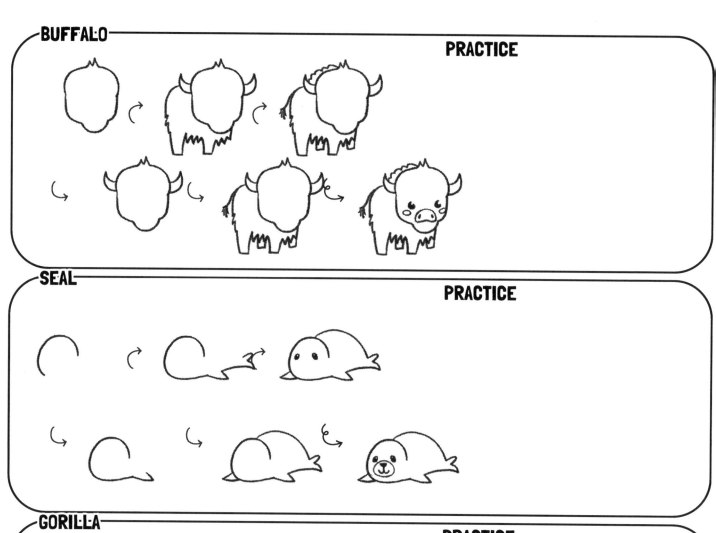

SEAL

GORILLA

TURKEY

DANCING·DUCK

GUINEA·PIG

OTTER

SNAKE

MOUSE

SLOTH

AARDVARK

OSTRICH

VULTURE PRACTICE

WARTHOG PRACTICE

ANTEATER PRACTICE

LOVABLE FOOD

TACO

CROISSANT

STRAWBERRY

PIZZA

APPLE

CHEESE

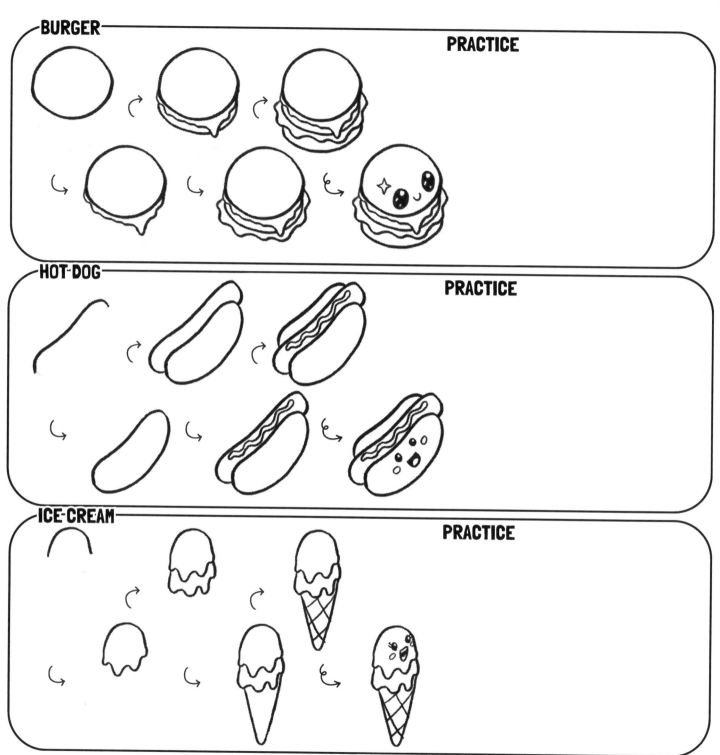

BURGER

PRACTICE

HOT-DOG

PRACTICE

ICE-CREAM

PRACTICE

PANCAKE

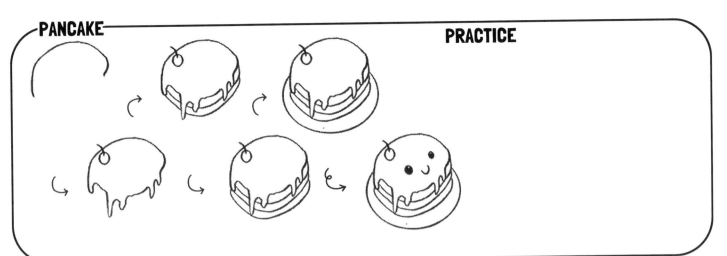

DONUT

WATERMELON

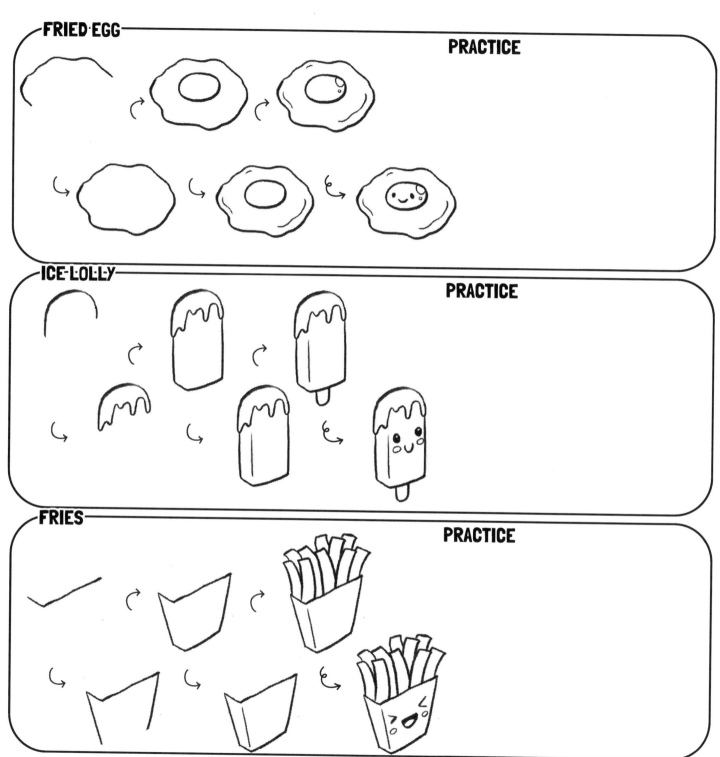

FRIED·EGG

ICE·LOLLY

FRIES

MUFFIN

CHOCOLATE-BAR

CARROT-CAKE

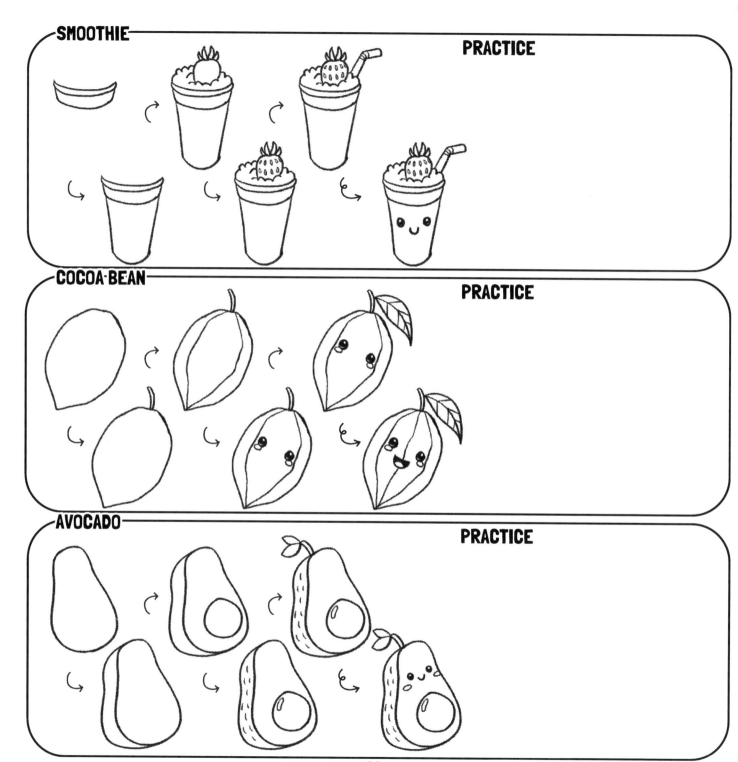

MILKSHAKE

COCONUT

ZUCCHINI

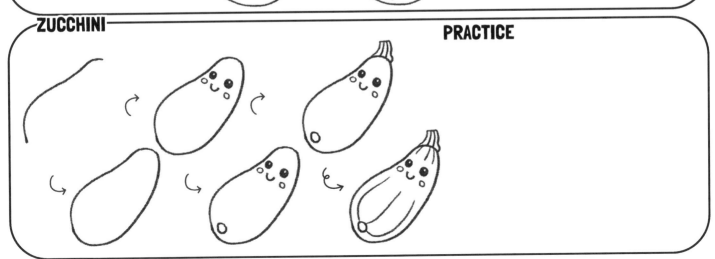

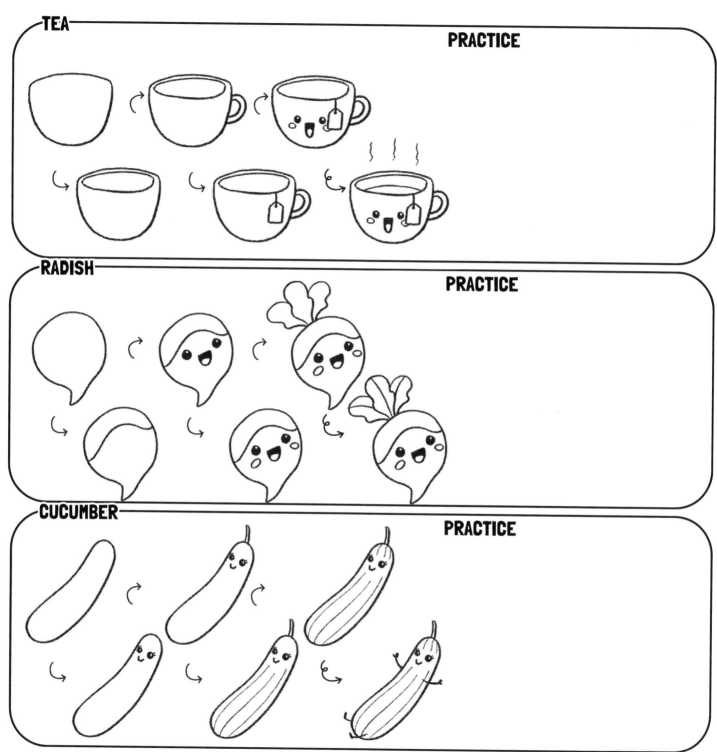

TEA

PRACTICE

RADISH

PRACTICE

CUCUMBER

PRACTICE

MILK

CARROT

PEAS

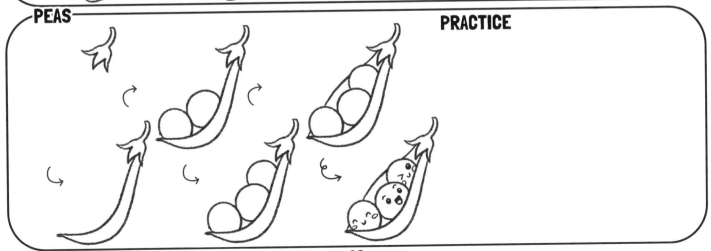

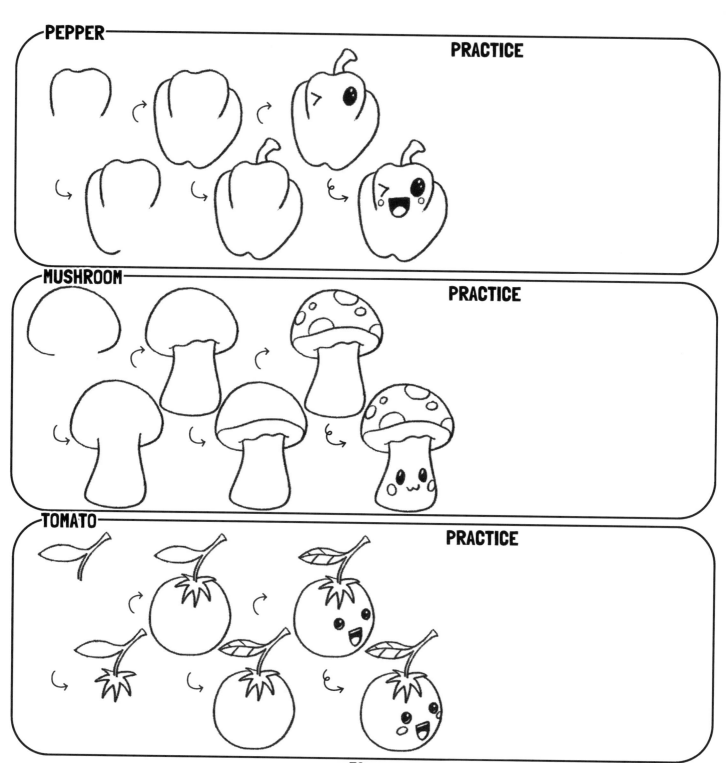

PEPPER

PRACTICE

MUSHROOM

PRACTICE

TOMATO

PRACTICE

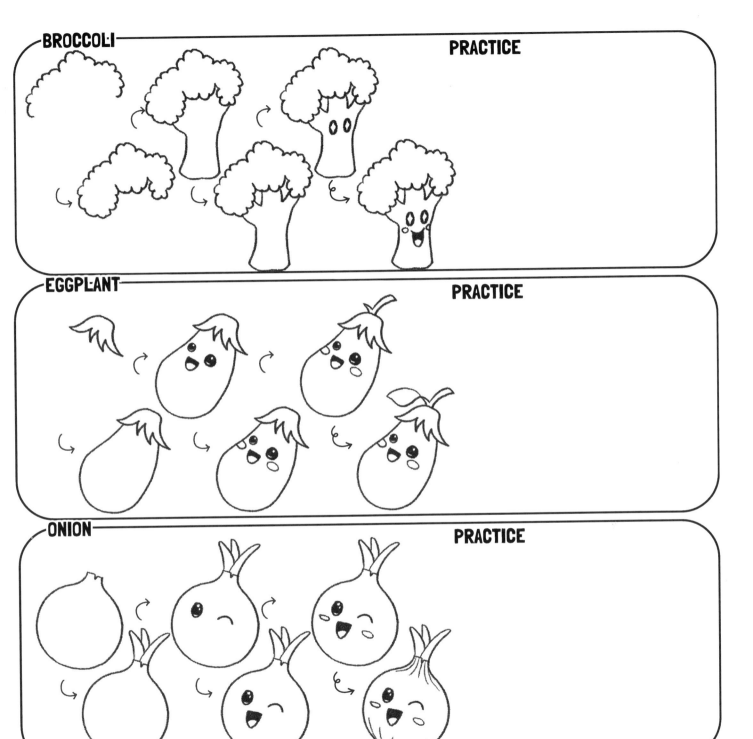

BROCCOLI

PRACTICE

EGGPLANT

PRACTICE

ONION

PRACTICE

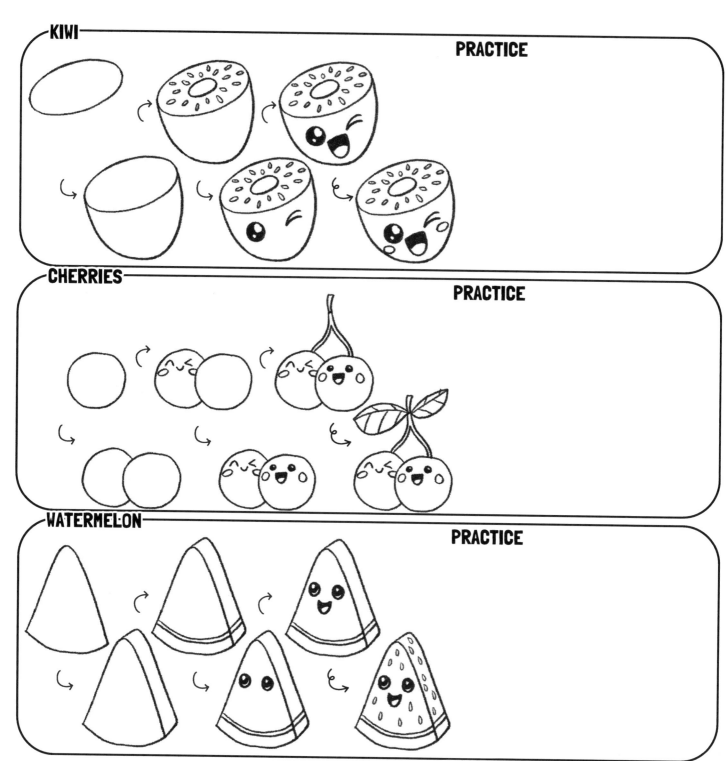

KIWI

CHERRIES

WATERMELON

LEMON

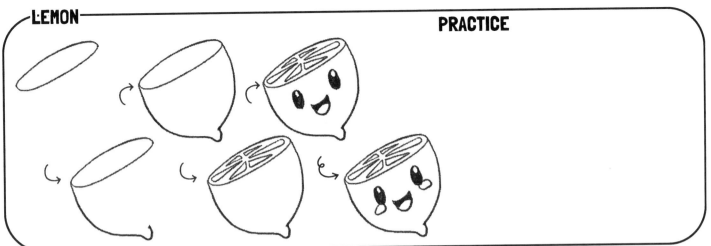

APPLE

PLUM

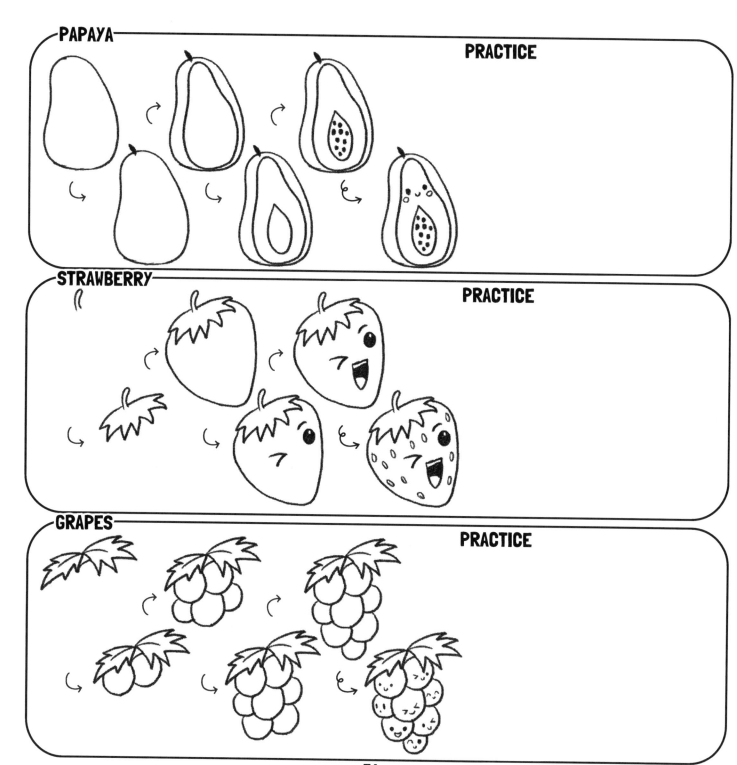

PAPAYA

STRAWBERRY

GRAPES

POMEGRANATE

PRACTICE

MANGO

PRACTICE

PUMPKIN

PRACTICE

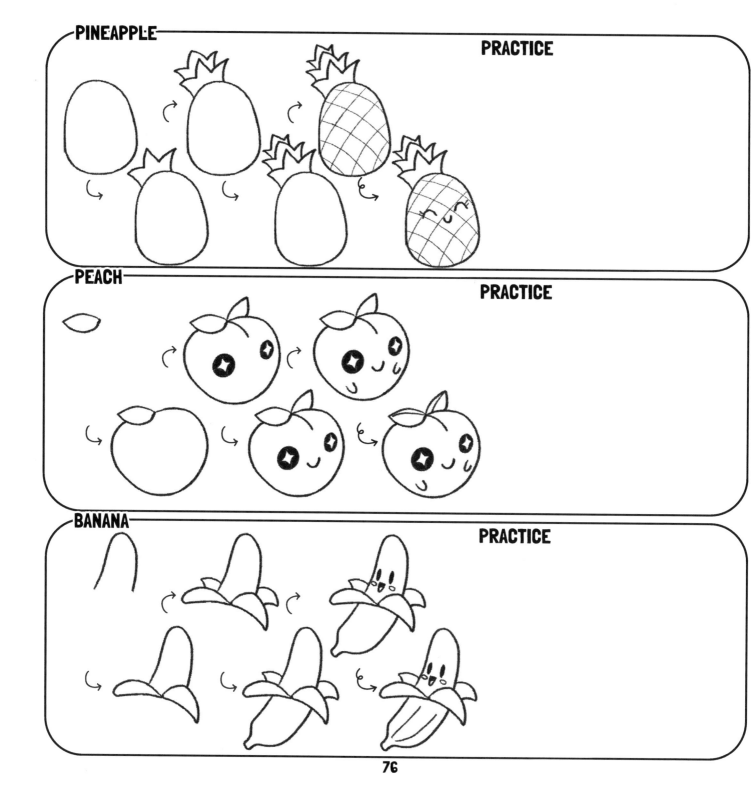

PINEAPPLE

PRACTICE

PEACH

PRACTICE

BANANA

PRACTICE

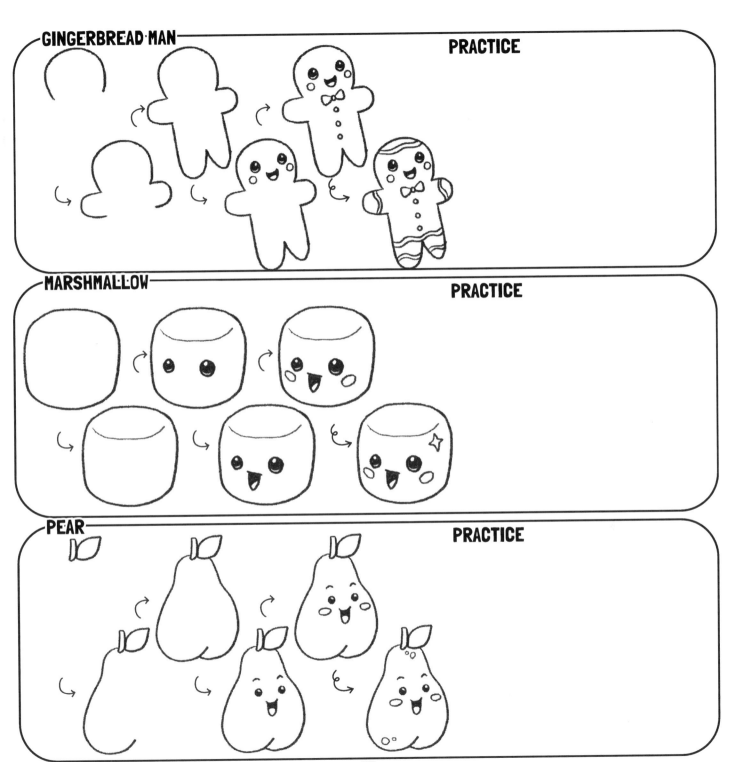

GINGERBREAD MAN

PRACTICE

MARSHMALLOW

PRACTICE

PEAR

PRACTICE

FRENCH·FRIES

RAMEN

SUSHI

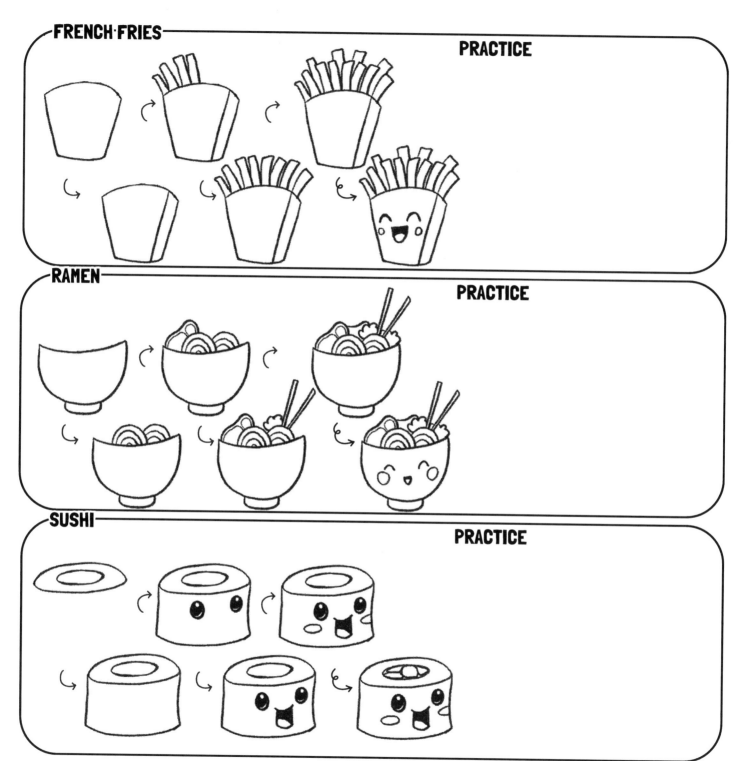

YOGURT

LAUGHING FRIED EGG

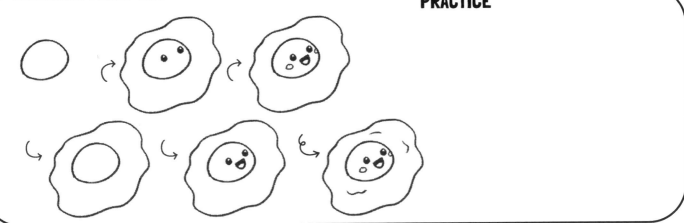

LATTE

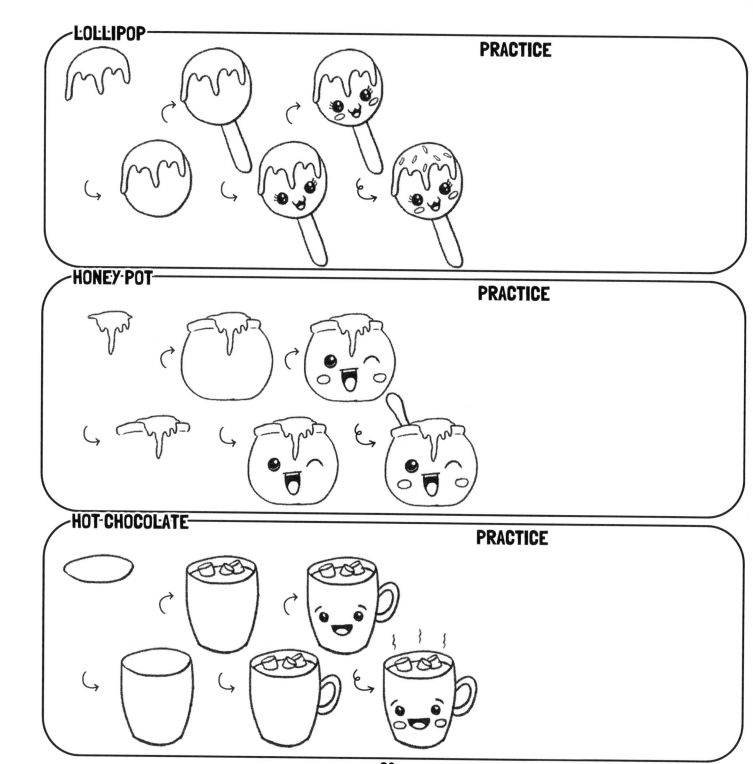

LOLLIPOP

HONEY POT

HOT CHOCOLATE

POPCORN

JELLY-JAR

SANDWICH

CHICKEN·NUGGETS

MACARONI·CHEESE

PEANUT·BUTTER

GRILLED CHEESE

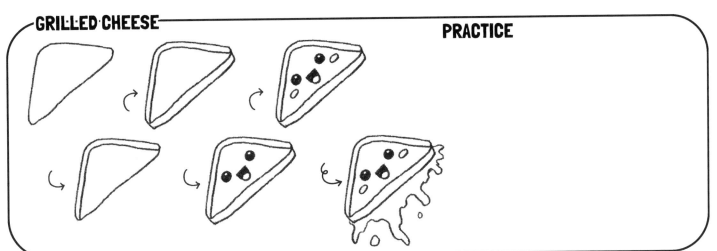

SPAGHETTI

MASH POTATO

AWESOME
SPORTS & TOYS

BASEBALL GLOVE

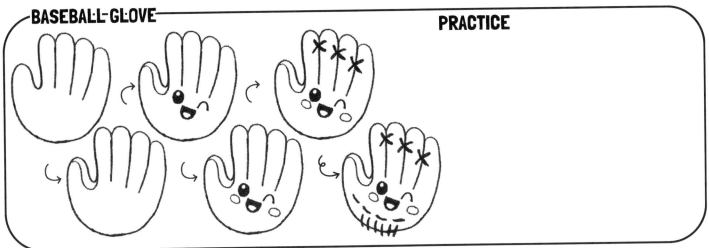

BASKETBALL

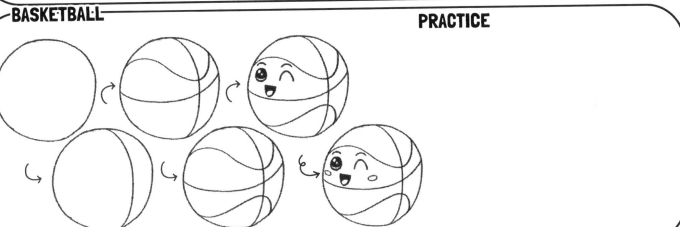

HOCKEY STICK

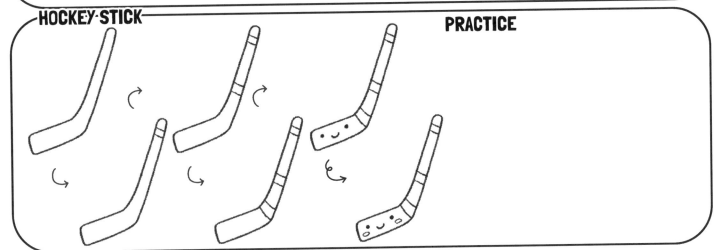

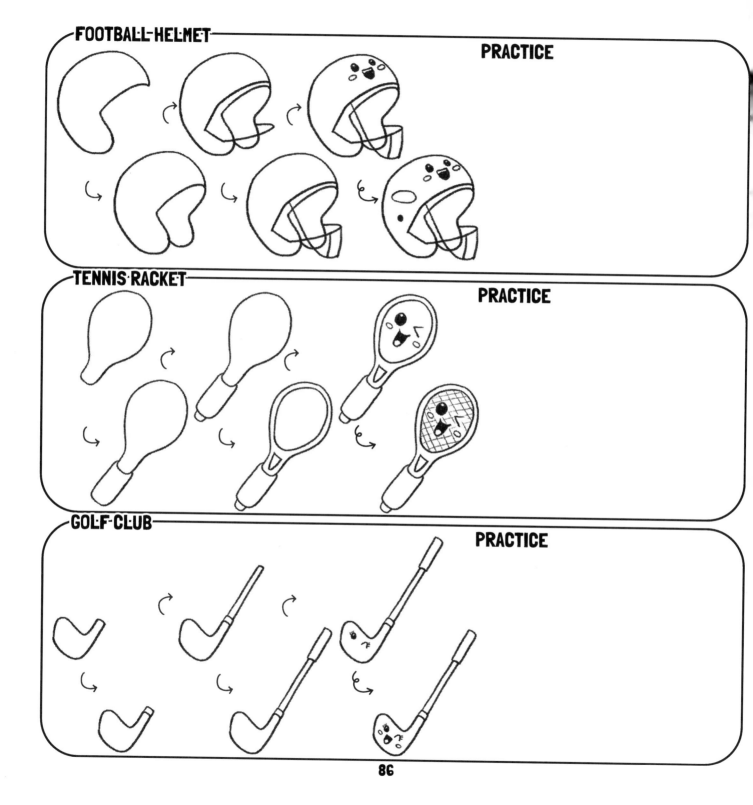

SOCCER BALL

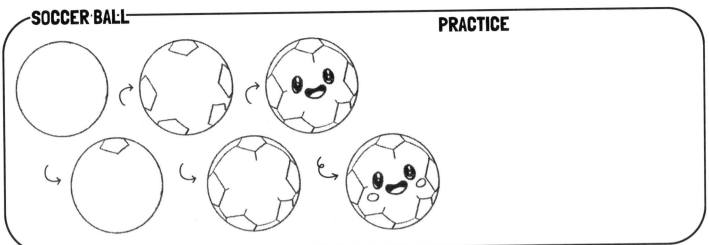

BOXING GLOVES

BASEBALL BAT

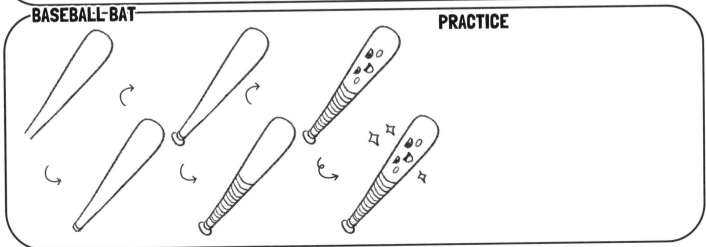

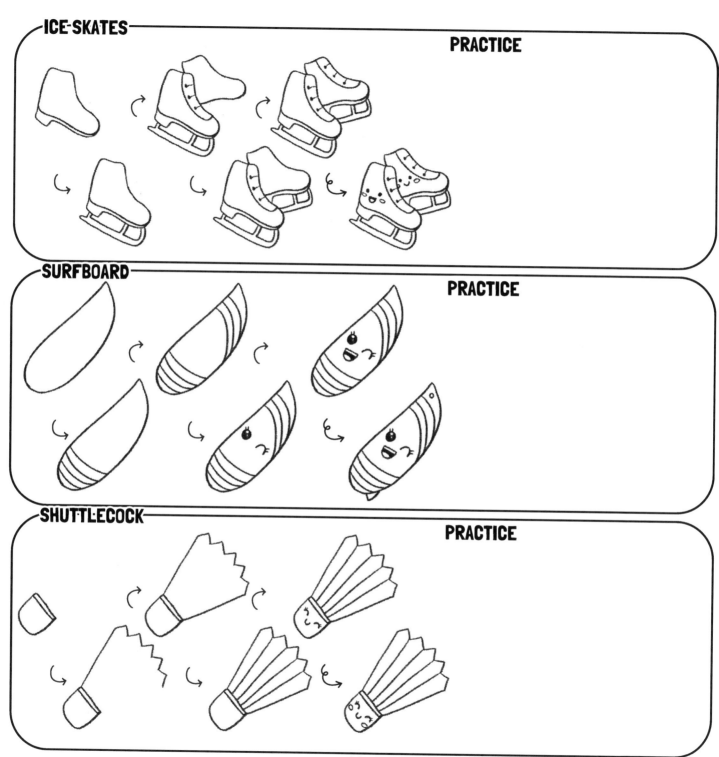

ICE-SKATES

PRACTICE

SURFBOARD

PRACTICE

SHUTTLECOCK

PRACTICE

PING PONG PADDLE

BOWLING BALL AND SKITTLE

BOW AND ARROW

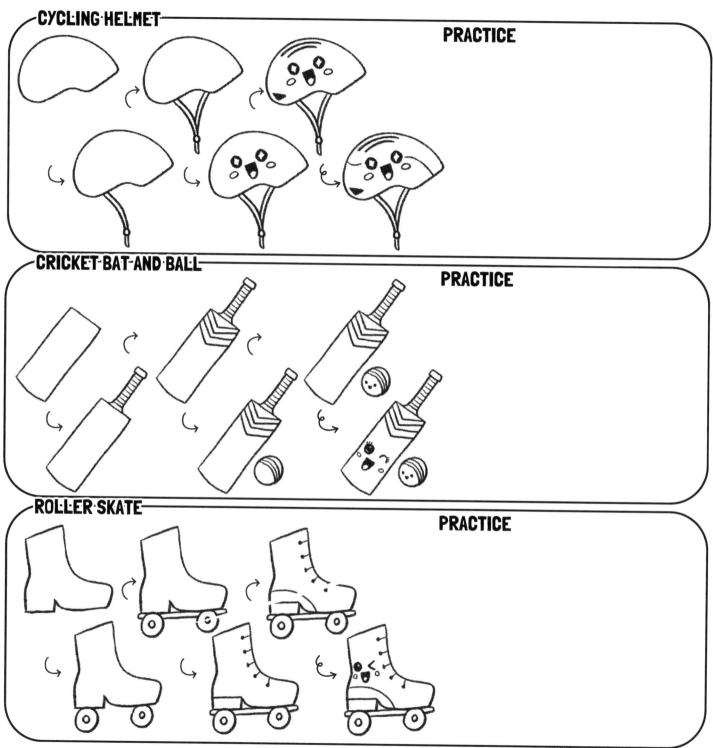

CYCLING·HELMET

CRICKET·BAT·AND·BALL

ROLLER·SKATE

TENNIS·BALL

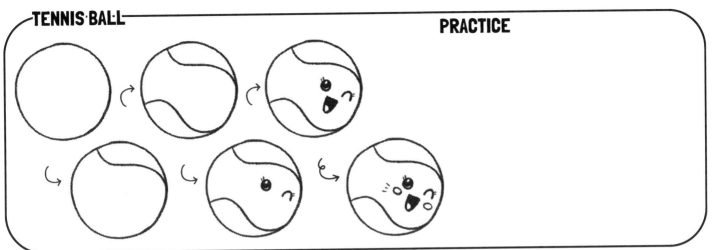

DIVING·FINS

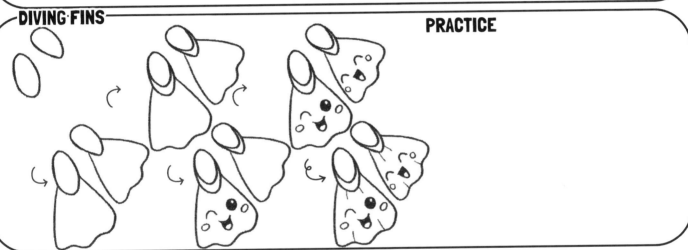

ARCHERY·TARGET

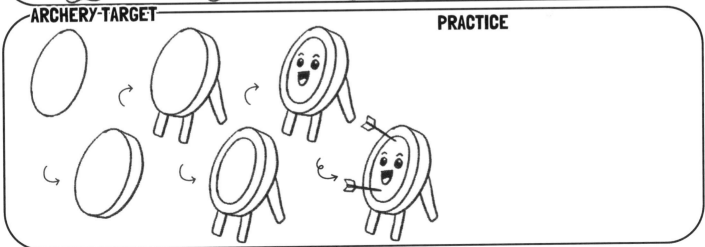

PRACTICE

PRACTICE

PRACTICE

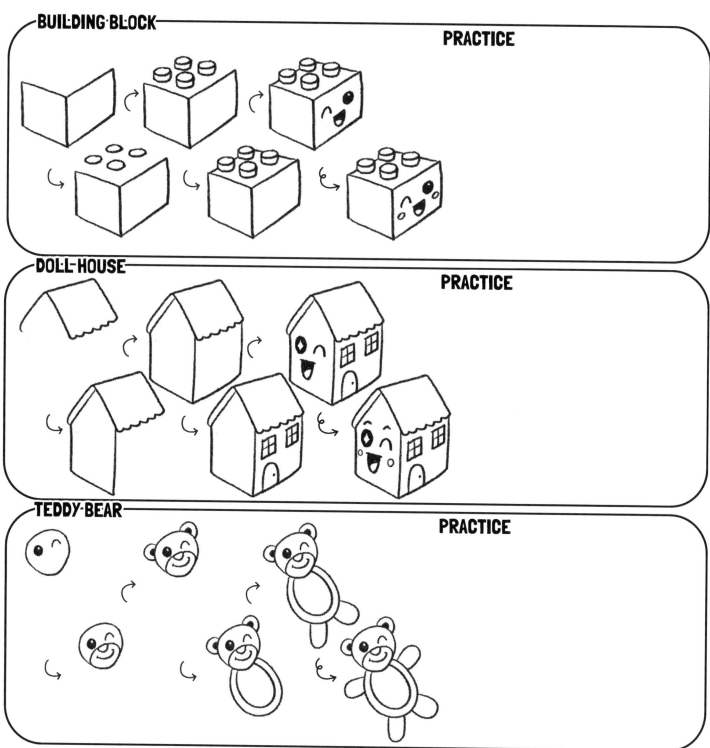

MAGICAL AND COOL!

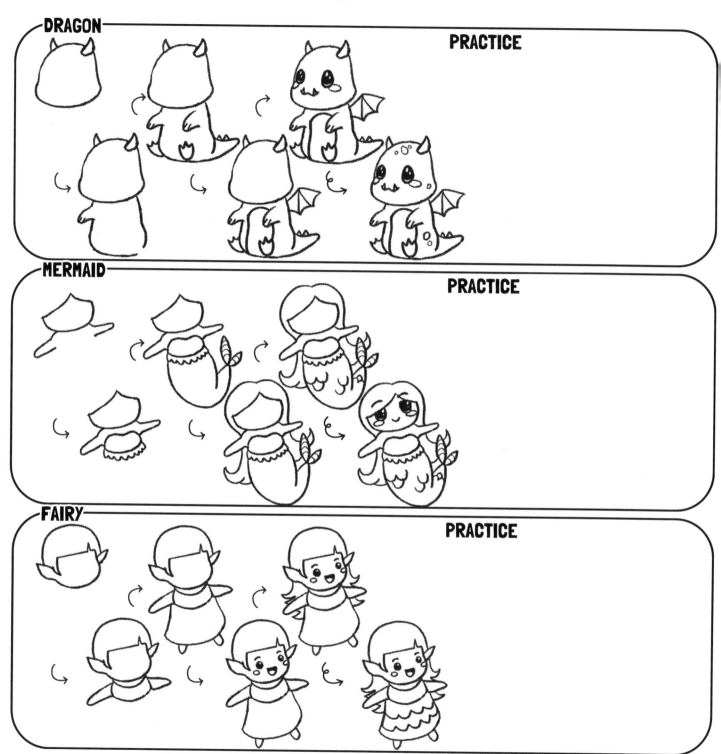

DRAGON

MERMAID

FAIRY

PEGASUS

WIZARD

ELF

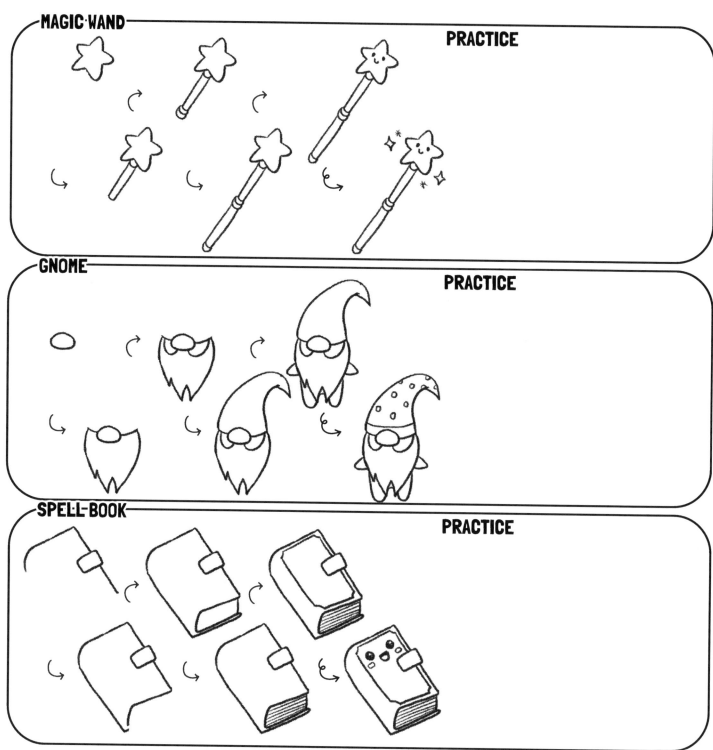

MAGIC·WAND
PRACTICE

GNOME
PRACTICE

SPELL·BOOK
PRACTICE

CRYSTAL BALL

TALKING TREE

MAGIC CARPET

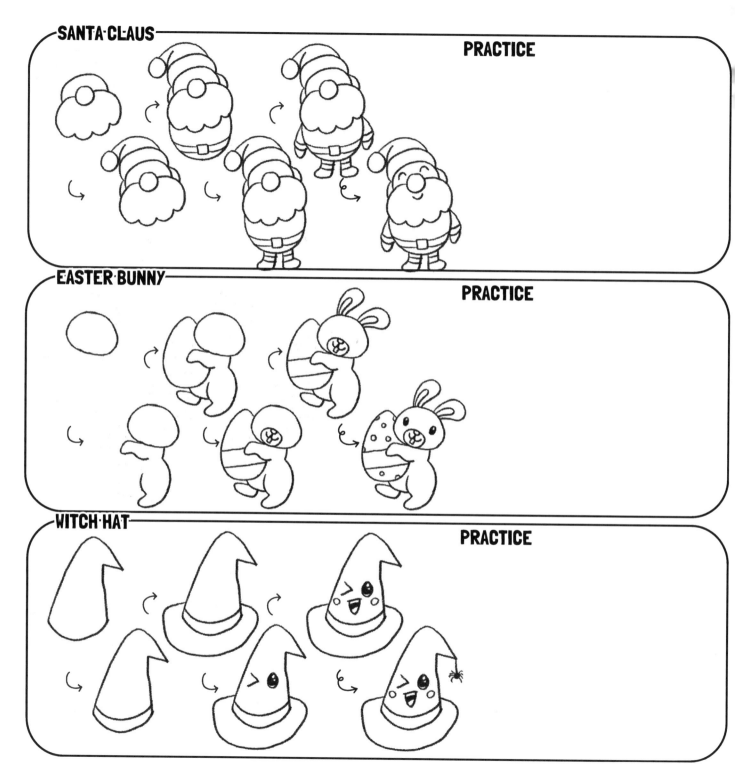

SANTA·CLAUS

PRACTICE

EASTER·BUNNY

PRACTICE

WITCH·HAT

PRACTICE

TREASURE CHEST

FRIENDLY GHOST

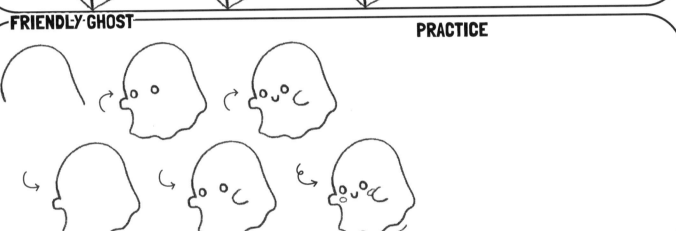

STARRY NIGHT

MAGIC·MIRROR

LEPRECHAUN

CENTAUR

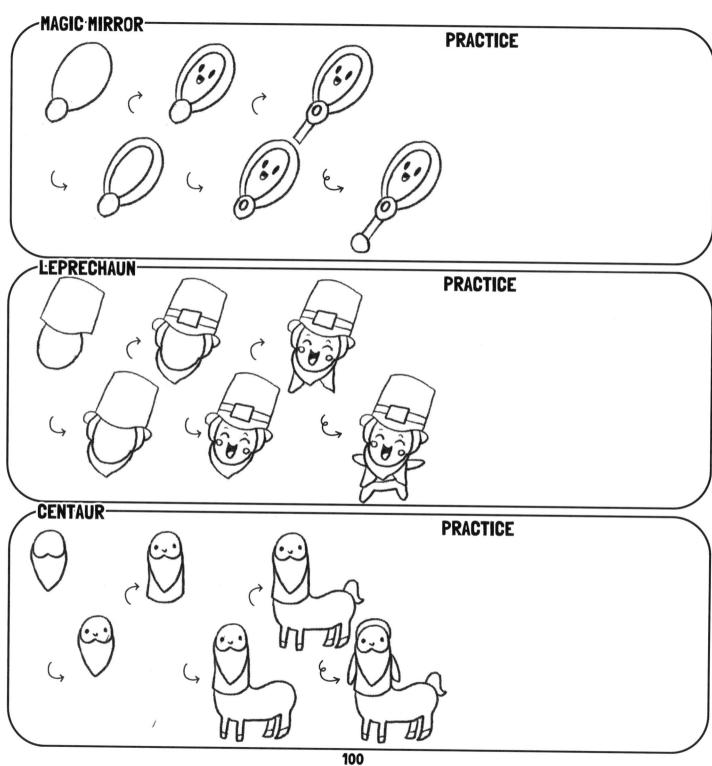

PIXIE

CATICORN

MAGICAL-HAT

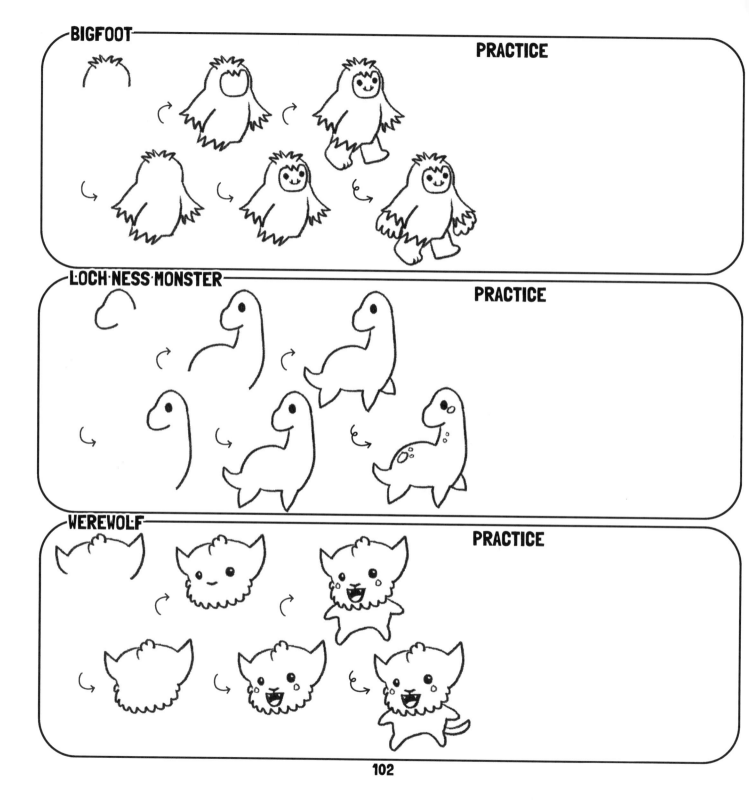

BIGFOOT

LOCH·NESS·MONSTER

WEREWOLF

MAGICAL LAMP

GOBLIN

DRAGON EGG

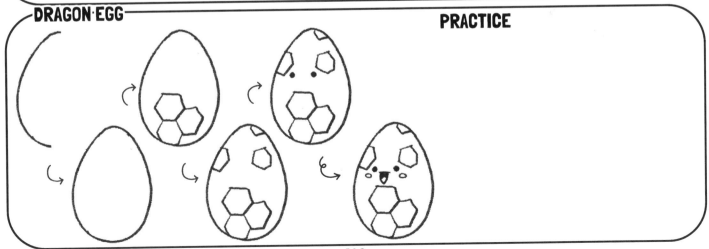

FLYING UNICORN

RAINBOW

PANDA DRINKING BOBA

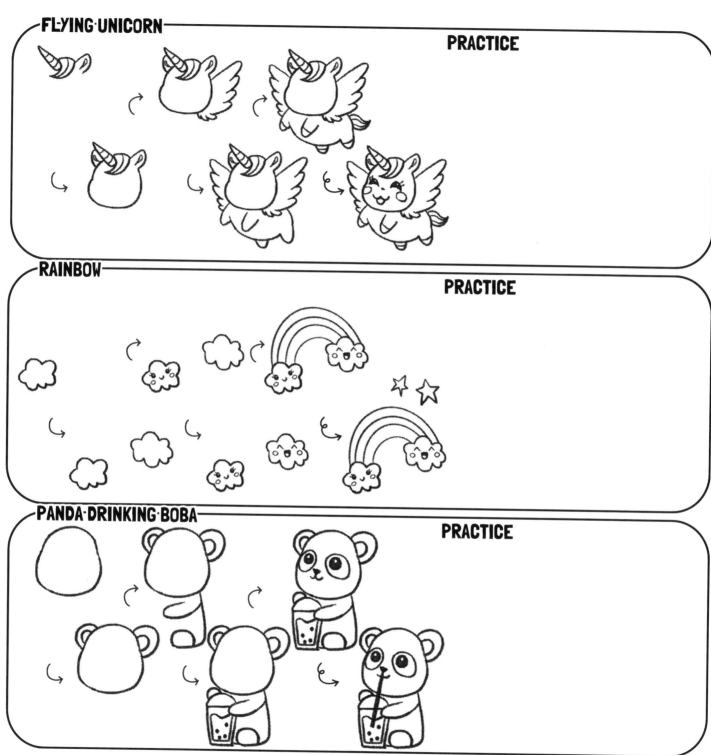

JUMPING·PANDA

UNICORN

DINOSAUR

FLYING·SERPENT

HAPPY·SHIP

MAGIC·KEY

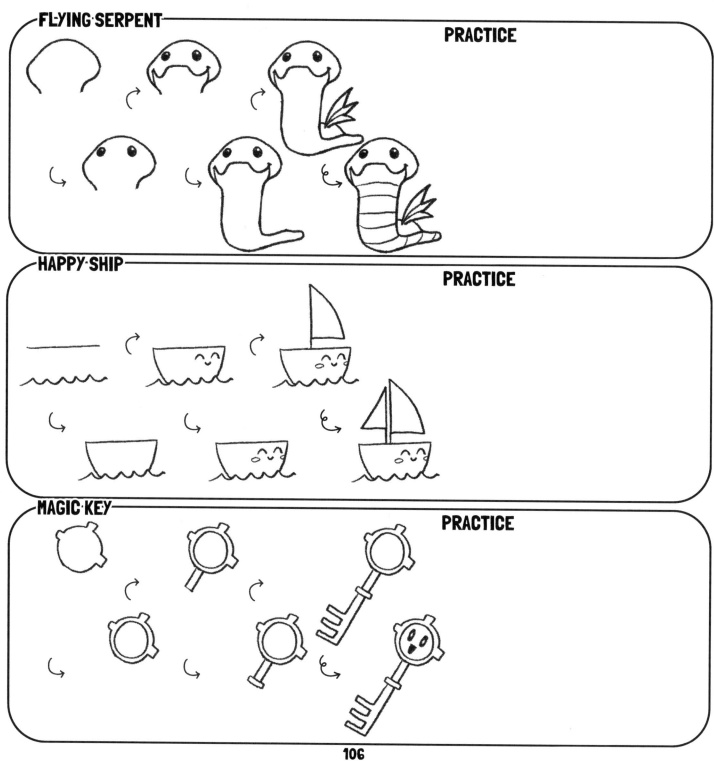

ENCHANTED CASTLE

CHIMERA

FOUNTAIN OF YOUTH

ENCHANTED SWORD

MAGIC SCROLL

CAULDRON

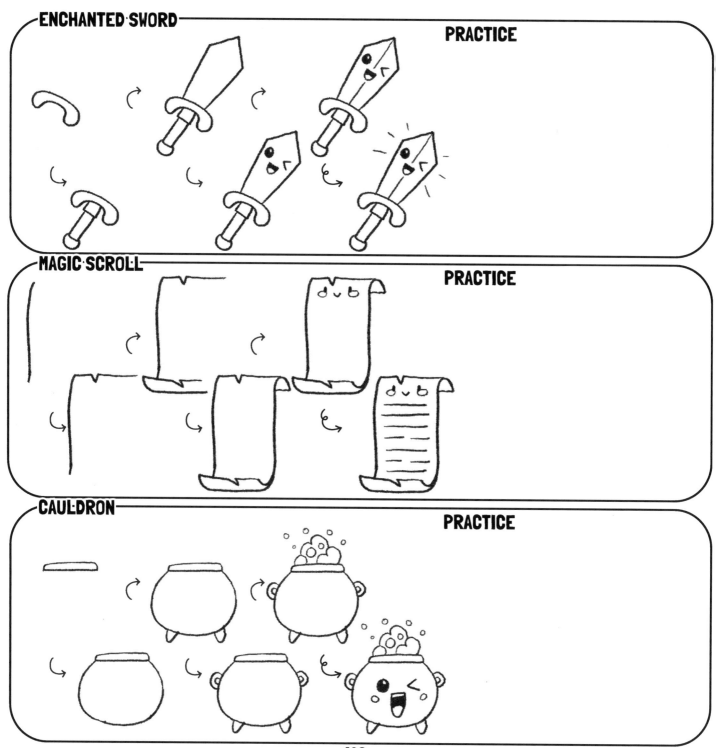

MAGICAL FLUTE
PRACTICE

KRAKEN
PRACTICE

PHOENIX
PRACTICE

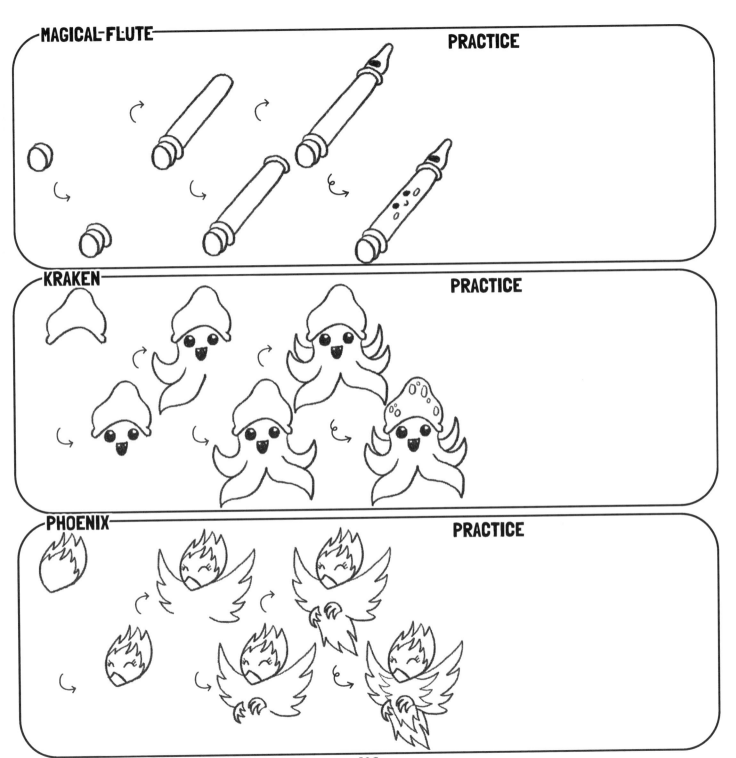

GRIFFIN

MINOTAUR

SPHINX

BASILISK

HYDRA

VAMPIRE

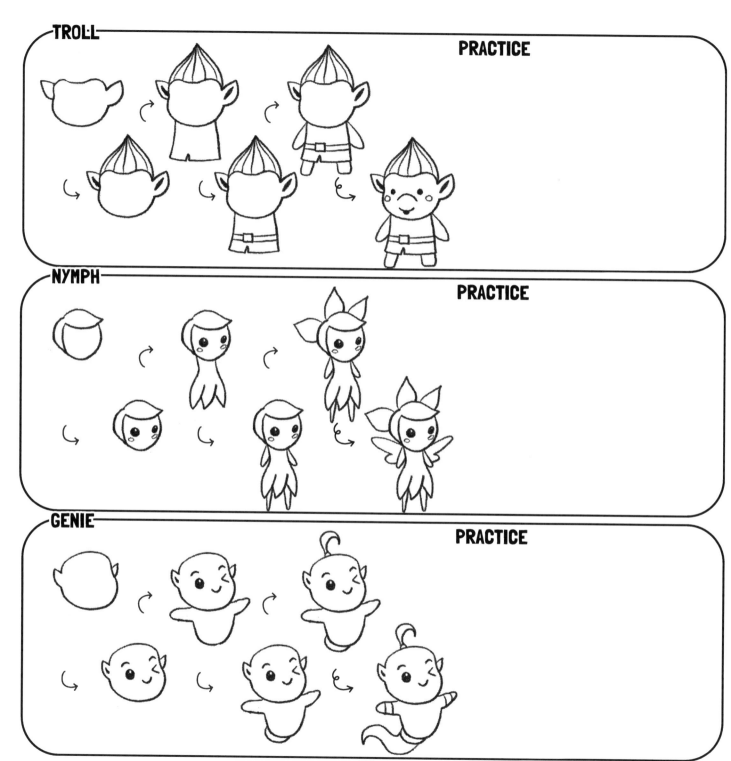

TROLL   PRACTICE

NYMPH   PRACTICE

GENIE   PRACTICE

AXOLOTL

CAT·DRINKING·BOBA

BANANA·CAT!

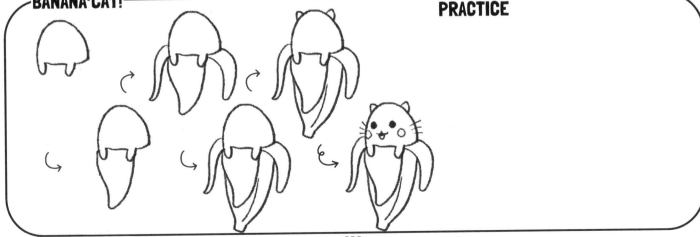

Made in the USA
Columbia, SC
07 June 2024